Into every life
a little Zen must fall

Into every life a little Zen must fall

A Christian philosopher looks
to Alan Watts and the East

Alan Keightley

Wisdom Publications London

First published in 1986

Wisdom Publications
23 Dering Street
London W1, England

© Alan Keightley

British Library Cataloguing in Publication Data
Keightley, Alan
    Into every life a little Zen must fall: a
    Christian philosopher looks to Alan Watts and
    the East.
    1. Christianity – Philosophy   2. Christianity
    and other religions – Zen Buddhism   3. Zen
    Buddhism – Relations – Christianity
    I. Title
    190   BR100
ISBN 0-86171-034-7

Set in Palatino 10½ on 13 point by Setrite of
Hong Kong, and printed and bound by Eurasia
Press of Singapore and Biddles of Guildford,
Surrey, on 85 gsm cream Graphic Text paper
supplied by Link Publishing Papers of West
Byfleet, Surrey.

Contents

For Paul – friend, son, philosopher of play

Foreword

FROM A SOCIOLOGICAL point of view one main function of religion has been to provide the cohesive principle of societies, from small pre-literate tribes to vast nationstates and empires. This social dimension of religion has had both constructive and destructive effects. On the one hand it has provided a common framework of meaning within which people have been able to interact with one another in accordance with accepted norms and to celebrate together life's joys and endure its miseries. But at the same time it has reinforced the 'us' against 'them' mentality within human conflict through the centuries, including today in the Middle East, the Persian Gulf area, the Punjab, and Northern Ireland. But although religion does thus still wield communal power, in the west its function as the principle of social cohesion has now largely been taken over by secular nationalism. Britain and the United States, France and West Germany, Canada and Sweden, and the other western societies, are now held together more by national sentiment, nationalistic mythology, and regional culture than by religion. Religion in the west has become less communal and more individual and personal.

This development, aided during the last two hundred years by other aspects of the emergence of the modern world, has given new scope to aspects of religion which had previously been suppressed in the west by politico-ecclesiastical institutions. In the medieval world individual mystical religion was marginalized. Today, particularly after the popular rediscovery of eastern spirituality, it has become a live option for many. The result is that, in Europe and the United States, as well as the slow decline of the main-line churches, and as well as the resurgence of fundamentalist Christianity, there has emerged a significant new religious option – a non-institutional spirituality of personal insight and experience, fed by the mystical traditions of both east and west.

One main source of this is Buddhism, and particularly Zen. Zen reveals the 'wondrous being' (in a famous Zen phrase) of the world experienced from an egoless point of view. The egoless consciousness is liberated from the inner agonies which so often make life a web of suffering; and is, in relation to others, a center of non-judgmental compassion. Zen is a way of experiencing the fact that samsara and nirvana are one: that is to say, eternal life is here and now. In its fullness Zen constitutes a religious tradition within which many people live and grow. But it can also be treated as a way of meditating and of seeing life which can become part of the practice of other traditions. There can be a Christian Zen (outlined in this book), a Jewish Zen, a Muslim Zen, a Hindu Zen, and so on. Or, as the title puts it, into every life a little Zen must fall.

It is a pleasure to commend this striking book by a western philosopher and theologian deeply influenced by Zen. One does not have to accept all Dr Keightley's philosophical interpretations – for example, his controversial interpretation of Wittgenstein – to find in these pages a lively and liberating application of the spirit of Zen. Here is religious writing which will speak to the condition of many who are alienated from institutional faith, and which can add a new dimension to faith within the other historical traditions.

JOHN HICK
Danforth Professor
Claremont Graduate School
  of Religion
California
August, 1985

Preface

WHENEVER I BORROW books from the local city library an assistant always asks me the same question; 'Can you identify yourself?' One day I shall summon up the courage to hold up a small mirror, look in it, and reply, 'Yes, that's me alright.' This would be a very Zen thing to do but I doubt whether it would carry weight with the young lady. She wants to know who people say I am, the role I am playing. The question, 'Who are we, *really*?' is one which runs through all the chapters of this book. The answer to any question is always another one – who wants to know? One of the reasons for writing this book is to express a little gratitude to some of the people who have questioned my own stereotypes of who we are beneath these stars.

Once in a while it really hits people that they don't have to experience the world in the way they have been told to. Cracks start to appear in the shell of their known world. My own shell cracked at eighteen while reading a book by the theologian Paul Tillich. It has cracked several times since then. People naturally see different things when their own shell goes. It is not always sensed as an enlightening experience. The Christian shell has broken for many people in our lifetime; there's nobody here but us chickens. One of the strongest impressions I have of a theological education in the late sixties is that of a college full of quietly desperate students on the search for something to keep them 'in.' The faces at early morning prayers were a dead giveaway – there's no one at home. Looking back now I think we were needlessly depressed. We had bought the conventional western view of who we are and were at the mercy of any new psychological or sociological theory of human identity. Not surprisingly many saw the dark and renounced the church. The evangelists turned into cacangelists, the bringers of bad news.

I want to say that the religious and philosophical news is fundamentally good, unbelievably good. Somehow the religious traditions have got themselves fouled up with dogma. There may be many things, it is assumed, we need to learn, but basically it's in the bag, it will yield no more mind-blowing secrets. That's a particular shell that ought to crack and it will if we allow ourselves to be surprised. I hope that this will come through in the pages which follow and will not be stifled by the academic hocus pocus where this rears its head. There is just no telling what people are going to make of a book. As a young teenager I often visited the local library in the days before we were asked philosophical questions about who we were. I borrowed very few books and read even fewer. I was overawed by any book which looked slightly more formidable than a football annual. I was daunted too by the great learning they surely contained. I had never seen an author and used to wonder where such demi-gods lived, imagining that they dwelt on some remote academic Sinai and handed down their wisdom to branch libraries for the benefit of mere mortals. I still feel twinges of anxiety and reverence when I see a large, tightly packed academic book, but the age of innocence has long since passed. I now realize at first hand that authors are human all too human and that many books are books about books.

If there is anything worthwhile in this book it derives from the people I have been privileged to know over the past few years. Some of these have been my own students and they know who they are. A few of these encounters have been very fleeting in the world historical sense but I remember them with great affection and gratitude. The seed of the present study probably had its origin several years ago in conversation with John Norris in the apocalyptic and shell cracking days of theological training. The conversation took place on a motor scooter through the streets of Bristol, England. We were discussing Martin Luther's theology at a steady twenty five miles an hour and in particular his observation that Adam's real sin was that he became theoretical about God. John may not remember this. He was steering at the time. Much that follows has been discussed into the wee small hours with my friends Graham and Linda Fergusson and in smokey bars with Neil McDonald. My thanks are also due to Professor John Hick and my colleague Geoff Wadhams for their kindness and interest. Stratford Caldecott was very encouraging at several stages in the book's development. Lynn McDaid and Robina Courtin at Wisdom have been lively and most helpful guides. My wife Joan has helped in countless ways. The book is dedicated to my son Paul who has taught me to be fascinated again by unimportant things.

ALAN KEIGHTLEY
King Edward VI College
Stourbridge
England

Acknowledgements

GRATEFUL ACKNOWLEDGEMENT is made to the following for permission to quote excerpts from previously published material:

Basil Blackwell for quotations from *Philosophical Investigations* and *Lectures and Conversations on Aesthetics, Psychology and Religious Belief*; both by Ludwig Wittgenstein.

Mrs Laura Huxley and Chatto & Windus for a quotation from *The Doors of Perception* by Aldous Huxley.

Hutchinson Publishing Group Ltd for a quotation from *Essays in Zen Buddhism* (first series) by D.T. Suzuki.

Krishnamurti Foundation Trust Ltd for quotations from the Krishnamurti books published by Victor Gollancz Ltd.

Peter Owen Ltd, London, for a quotation from *Siddhartha* by Hermann Hesse, translated by Hilda Rosner.

Princeton University Press for quotations from *Philosophies of India* by Heinrich Zimmer, ed. Joseph Campbell, Bollingen Series 26, copyright 1951.

Random House, Inc., Alfred A. Knopf, Inc. for quotations from *Beyond Theology*, *In My Own Way* and *Behold The Spirit*; all by Alan Watts.

Introduction
Technical philosophers and the Dharma bums

AN OLD JEWISH LADY once asked her grandson what he was going to be when he grew up. The young man replied, 'A doctor of philosophy.' His grandmother said, 'That's wonderful my boy, but what sort of a disease is philosophy?' It's the element of truth in the story which makes it amusing. The word philosophy does have the smell of the laboratory about it these days. In a recent book Jacob Needleman has tried to put the heart back into philosophy. He warns of the mistake of confusing the standard 'problems of philosophy' – freewill, knowing other minds, etc. – with real philosophy. These problems are 'only the fossilized remains of what were once living and breathing 'creatures.' Official philosophy, a sort of paleontology of the mind, lays out these bones and fragments and reconstructs gigantic skeletons called 'philosophical arguments,' which are housed in museums called philosophy departments and philosophical texts.... The 'problems of philosophy' are only the tracks left by the questions of philosophy – something that has long since moved on, and is still moving within every serious human being.'[1] In a similar vein, William Earle has written a very amusing and tart account of how the noble discipline of philosophy has committed suicide. He describes the nine to five technical philosopher who only wishes to be clear about little things and who would wear a white laboratory coat if he could get away with it.[2] The word theology has suffered too. It is a word frequently used by British politicians to describe something which is irrelevant to the matter in hand.

As far as credibility goes the gurus of the east fare just as badly. They are often regarded as pompous phonies. Gita Mehta debunked the gurus in a humourous way in the aptly titled book *Karma Cola*. More than one journalist has succumbed to substituting Bagwash for Bhagwan. Sometimes trivia and pomposity are combined when a westerner plays guru. Some readers may have heard of the grey haired lady who climbed three flights of stairs, opened a carved mahogany door and walked into an exotically furnished reception room. A gong sounded and out of a cloud of incense appeared a beautiful brunette Oriental: 'Do you wish to meet with His Omnipotence, the wise, all-knowing, all-seeing guru, Maharishi Naru?' 'Yeah,' said the old woman, 'Tell Irving his mama is here from the Bronx.'

We have then a picture of the dessicated philosopher who knows the words but not the music and is all rattle and click. At the other extreme is the vagrant philosopher, the dharma bum dishing out enlightenment by the shovel full. These are caricatures of course. Yet they do point to two great areas of religious and philosophical experience which are mutually neglectful, if not contemptuous, of each other. This is not just an issue for those involved professionally in these matters. All of us are involved. This book attempts to involve the so-called ordinary person in the issues at stake. I shall use the remainder of this introduction to set out the general course of the discussion and prepare the reader for what is to come.

MAVERICK PHILOSOPHERS AND THE WILD SCIENCE

When this book was in its early stages I was relieved to discover that it spoke to the condition of at least one person. A friend of mine, after reading one of the first drafts, explained that he had grown up on the writings of Krishnamurti and Alan Watts but had not dared to confess his interest throughout the time he studied for a philosophy degree at one of England's old established universities. Those two philosophers simply would not have been taken seriously. Professional philosophy can certainly be as parochial as anything else. A professor of philosophy I had often went through the charade of looking behind curtains and doors before a lecture in case an Oxford philosopher was lurking about. However, my friend's hesitancy to mention Watts and Krishnamurti points to a much wider issue than the fashions within western philosophy.

In a sentence, I shall attempt to put some aspects of the straight kind of western philosophical thinking on speaking terms with the experiences which emerged through the development of eastern inspired consciousness movements of the past few decades. Several separate issues will arise in the course of the discussion but these will have that common background. I have concentrated on Watts and Krishnamurti on the eastern side and Ludwig Wittgenstein on the western. Krishnamurti and Watts addressed themselves to the west but they are philosophers who have also imbibed a great deal of eastern thinking. I shall be concerned with Alan Watts in particular. His approach offers a very fruitful meeting place for nine to five technical philosophy and the kind that is written after dark. Writing in 1972, he commented that he needed to wait a decade for the right perspective on his own contribution in the field of philosophy and religion. He died in 1973 and we are deprived of the personal assessment he would have made just about now. This present study could be seen as an attempt to do, in a very small way, what he would have done with far greater depth and wit. In his autobiography, *In and Out the Garbage Pail*, the founder of gestalt therapy, Fritz Perls, comments on his work with Alan Watts and observes, 'Seldom has anyone spoken so elegantly and so generously about the *non*-verbal.' Watts' writings acted as a catalyst for many individuals who applied some of his ideas to areas outside of Watts' own sphere of interest or competence. Some of his major concerns can be traced in more developed form in the recent writings of thinkers like E.F. Schumacher, Fritjof Capra and Marilyn Ferguson. The present study hopefully connects Watts with areas in which his ideas have been largely ignored, namely, western theology and philosophy. In the chapters which follow there are only occasional biographical references. Anyone interested in reading about the enigmatic Watts and his joker lifestyle can consult his autobiography and a recently completed study by Monica Furlong, *Genuine Fake: A Biography of Alan Watts.*[3]

Alan Watts and Krishnamurti are both leading pioneers on what Theodore Roszak has called the Aquarian frontier, the religious revival in western society which is taking place outside the confines of institutional religion. Roszak surveys the vast variety of growth points on the frontier, many of which have jaw-breaking labels – etherealized healing, eupsychian therapies, organicism, neo-primitivism and paganism, psychotronics, etc.[4] Watts and Krishnamurti belong to those areas on the frontier which have an awakened interest in eastern religions. In chapter one I have discussed some of the basic issues which have emerged out of the so-called new religious consciousness and which are relevant to this study. In his own analysis Roszak attempts to locate what he calls centres of consensus on the Aquarian frontier. One of these seems to me to be of fundamental importance and lies in the background of much of what follows; 'We are leaving behind all religions, philosophies, and worldviews that exhaust themselves in language – in doctrines, catechisms, abstract analysis, academic head trips.... We are learning how to stop being compulsive *explainers.*'[5] We are witnessing the appearance of a new sensibility, a form of religious experience which is somehow beyond faith and belief in doctrinal statements. Roszak believes that we are seeing the possibility of a shift in consciousness fully as epoch-making as the appearance of speech.

By now we are beginning to develop more stable perspectives on these new movements. Charles Tart, for example, has done substantial work on altered states of consciousness, the so-called wild science.[6] The universities were always ready to study the new movements sociologically but now there are signs that the aquarians are being taken seriously for what they *say*. Jacob Needleman in particular has tried to expose mainstream philosophy to the new religions and the esoteric traditions. In his recent book, *The Heart of Philosophy*, he argues that we live in a time of metaphysical repression which has stifled the love of meaning, a phrase which, he reminds us, is the true definition of philosophy. In his preface to *Understanding the New Religions* Needleman recalls the first class he attended as a student of philosophy. When the instructor asked the class what they expected from the course Needleman responded enthusiastically, 'I want to know the meaning of life.' He goes on:

> I will never forget the silence that followed. At first, I simply did not understand it; I assumed the teacher was waiting for me to say more, and so I went on talking while vaguely beginning to suspect that something was not quite right.
>
> I don't remember anything of what I said, only that it was all centred around the question 'Why are we here?'
>
> Suddenly, I noticed that the teacher was smiling. I almost said 'sneering,' but that would probably be an exaggeration. At the same time, I noticed my classmates shaking their heads and I heard some snickering as well.
>
> I stopped cold.
>
> 'Go on, go on.' I was told.
>
> Bewildered and frightened, I did try to go on and speak about all the questions that had been troubling me, but my voice was hollow and I soon had to stop.
>
> After another terrible pause, the teacher said (and this I remember precisely):
>
> 'Yes – well, that is exactly what philosophy is *not* about. You are *not* going to get psychiatric help here (great laughter), or religious guidance (more laughter). No, you are going to be taught

what it means to think clearly and well, to examine your presuppositions, to criticize and argue. That is philosophy.'[7]

Needleman went on to say that such an answer should no longer be given. In his more recent study he claims that there is a 'yearning in the human heart that is nourished only by real philosophy and without this nourishment man dies as surely as if he were deprived of food and air. But this part of the human psyche is not known or honoured in our culture.'[8] The sense of philosophy as an awakener of the real, as that which deals with the truly gut-level questions of life has been lost. This is presumably why the consciousness movements could find so few channels in the philosophical establishment through which they could find expression. This accounts too for the popularity of maverick philosophers like Alan Watts and Krishnamurti with their massive readership. The churches too, identified as they are with the secular zeitgeist, have failed to understand the reemergence of religion in its new and mystical forms. We do not expect the professional philosopher to give us a meaning for life and neither, it seems, do many expect it to be provided by the representatives of western religion. There are versions of the religions readily available but these often merely confirm the conventions and rarely disrupt the normal state of consciousness.

Having said this it is also true that all is not dross. Just as there are signs that the philosophical establishment is opening up so too are there signs that the theologians are waking from their dogmatic slumbers. At the academic level thinkers like the Canadian Islamic scholar Cantwell Smith and the British theologian John Hick are pioneering a global theology.[9] There is definitely more openness now on the part of the religions to receive from each other. Theodore Roszak reminds us that Aquarius is the bringer of water in the midst of a parched and dying wasteland. Refreshment can come from the oddest quarters as Christ discovered when he received a cup of cold water from that disreputable foreigner, the woman of

Samaria. In chapters two and three I shall discuss the living water in the writings of Krishnamurti and Alan Watts which may suggest ways in which it can flow into the arid areas of religion, philosophy and the spirituality of just anyone who is parched by the secularity of western culture.

THE WESTERN CONNECTION

I hope that these first few pages have set the mood for the first third of the book. In the second third of the study I pay more attention to the western religious and philosophical scene in its more traditional forms. In some ways the past few decades have been depressing ones for religion so far as philosophical discussions are concerned. Religion does not have the dignity of being just plain wrong. Religion, we are told, is simply misusing language. Believers certainly seem to be on the defensive in modern philosophy and there is a definite smell of the courtroom about many of the debates. Take, for example, the whole question of the justification of religious belief. The title of Antony Flew's book, *The Presumption of Atheism*, accurately conveys the flavour. Atheism is a presumption which sets the context for any religious case which may be offered, in a similar way to that of the innocence – until proved guilty – of the accused in English law. The religious case has to be justified. At least this seems to be the general consensus. The very format of some philosophical journals resemble the printed reports of the quarter sessions.

This is not the whole story however. During this same period there has developed a substantial challenge to the courtoom approach. This development is based on the work of Ludwig Wittgenstein and his followers. If this movement has a motto it is 'Don't think. Look!'[10] If we get behind our deeply rooted assumptions about what religion is supposed to be we will see that many of these assumptions are wrong. Religion is autonomous and has no need to justify itself before a greater authority. There is no charge to answer. No philosophical courtroom is wide enough to put belief and unbelief side by side and so judge between them. If we fail to realize this there is a miscarriage of philosophical justice. Words and activities are taken from their natural, religious setting and placed in a context quite inappropriate to their true sense and meaning. The following statement by Wittgenstein makes the point:

> When philosophers use a word – 'knowledge,' 'being,' 'object,' 'I,' 'proposition,' 'name' – and try to grasp the *essence* of the thing, one must always ask oneself: is the word ever actually used in this way in the language-game which is its original home?
>
> What *we* do is to bring words back from their metaphysical to their everyday use.[11]

I shall pick up the passage again but a few comments here may help those unfamiliar with the issues to orientate themselves for what is to follow. The 'everyday' is the true, natural use and the 'metaphysical' the philosopher's distorted use. The question is, of course, what religion is like when it is truly in context, at home. Wittgenstein's followers have offered their own views about this and have evoked a great deal of controversy in the process. Their analyses may be judged as right or wrong but this does not affect the more general point about the impossibility of conceiving a wider context for judging between fundamental world pictures. To take one of the examples from Wittgenstein's list above; is there a general consensus about the meaning of 'I,' common to both believers and unbelievers? We could ask the same question of the other examples in the passage – knowledge, object, being, etc. Many religious views involve a complete transformation of what it normally means to be alive, whether or not these are thought to be meaningful to any particular individual. There is no neutral understanding of self and world which provides a basis for a philosopher to act as judge and jury over those who allegedly misuse them.

Wittgenstein's philosophy seems to me to be the most promising for establishing some kind of dialogue between the philosophical establishment and those pushing out the borders of the Aquarian frontier. Readers may grant this possibility if they can see the relevance of Krishnamurti's philosophy for the verification debate in a passage such as the following:

> 'What does it mean to agree or disagree?' Krishnamurti asks. It means that one has matched what one has heard against one's own thoughts, and found that it either conforms to these thoughts or does not. In either case, one has learned nothing new; one has either reinforced a previous opinion or rejected a new thought. When our opinions are reinforced, we call it verification, but this is very far from the verification which is demanded by Krishnamurti.[12]

Chapters three and four attempt to establish a dialogue between Wittgenstein's approach and the kind of religious philosophy advocated by Watts and Krishnamurti.

THE RELIGION OF NO RELIGION

By the time we reach the final third of the book the point of the title should be clear. Our religion, our philosophy, our lives are changed when we allow a little Zen to fall. We have a new dimension of consciousness. There is no exposition of Zen as such in what follows. There are many books which say what it is, or rather say what it isn't. Nevertheless, a few observations here may be useful. To have no Zen is to be bamboozled by concepts; to confuse the description of the world with the world itself. To have Zen is to be in a state of pure sensation. It is to be freed from the grip of concepts, to see through them. This is *not* the same as rejecting conceptual thinking. Thoughts and words are in the world and are as natural as flowers. It is a mistake therefore to think that Zen is anti-intellectual. Many Zen teachers have been great intellectuals, not least R.H. Blyth and D.T. Suzuki of recent times. Zen may certainly appear to put down conceptual thinking when the masters try to dehypnotize us from our attachment to thought. What matters is our awareness of what *is*, the world in its thusness. As the Zen teachers say, it is to drink water and know *for yourself* that it is cold.

In the light of the Zen approach the traditional religions change – and I would say deepen – their meanings. Religion appears more to do with the transformation of consciousness than correct things to believe. In one sense consciousness must always be an unknown. It is a constant in our experiences; it is the condition of our experiencing all things. Therefore, it can never become an object of knowledge. If religion is to do with states and qualities of consciousness then the standard philosophical approaches to religion in the west just will not do any more. We could say that Zen is, to use Frederic Spiegelberg's words, the religion of no religion. In its light the religions are allowed to be themselves. In chapter five I shall discuss some of the familar Christian doctrines from a point of view influenced by Zen. It is only fair for me to admit right away that many orthodox Christians will find that chapter a contentious one. The late Jacob Bronowski, though speaking from outside the Christian tradition in his *The Ascent of Man*, probably wrote for many Christians when he said that he was saddened by the retreat in the west from knowledge into Zen Buddhism with its 'falsely profound questions.' Bronowski went on to say that 'no beliefs can be built up in this century that are not based on science as the recognition of the uniqueness of man, and a pride in his gifts and works.' If Bronowski's remarks are at all representative of the western intellectual they demonstrate vividly just how deep the chasm is which separates him from the Zen masters. One can only imagine how phrases like 'uniqueness of man' and 'pride in his gifts and works' would ring in Suzuki's ears. Perhaps Suzuki would have been as generous as the young man in the following anecdote. A middle class American father despaired of the way his hippie son spent his days sitting around contemplating his return to the Buddhist Void and shouted, 'Son, don't you realize that you are going to amount to *nothing*!' His son said, 'Gee dad, you really do understand!'

Speaking for myself I find Bronowski's remarks depressing. They seem to express a blindness to the speaker's own questionable assumptions about the world. Yet, I would say, they are typical of what you are likely to hear in the universities and the streets. How could such a state of mind even begin to approach the mysteries of religion? It is just too superficial and concept bound. As R.H. Blyth asks provocatively; 'How deep are you and your words? If they are shallower than mine, you can't understand my answer.'[13] Perhaps this is why the Buddha was not, it is said, interested in arguing for the existence of God or the gods. There is a story that someone once approached the Buddha and asked him if there was a God. Buddha refused to answer despite the man's desperate pleadings. The man persisted and eventually the Buddha said, 'Okay. Stay with me for one year without speaking and then ask me your question.' Some of the Buddha's followers overheard the conversation and shouted to the enquirer, 'Don't fall for that one! We fell for it. In a year's time you won't want to ask the question.' In other words, the question would disappear as an intellectual puzzle. The man would have *become* the mystery. To quote R.H. Blyth again; 'Every answer is circumscribed by its question, the smell by the nose. Can the eye see itself? When this happens we have the state of Zen.'[14] A truly enlightened answer simply cannot be understood by the unenlightened state of mind.

There is a story from the Hindu tradition which makes a similar point. An Upanishadic teacher is asked, 'How many gods are there?' He replies,

'There are as many gods as there are in the hymns
to the Vishwa-devas – 3,300.'
'Yes, but how many are there *really*?'
'Thirty three.'

'How many?'
'Six.'
'How many?'
'Three.'
'No, how many really?'
'Two.'
'How many?'
'One and a half.'
'Now come on. How many really?'
'One.'

If we ask beyond this question the teacher would, it is said, beat a drum. The questioner would be asking for a verbal answer in dualistic terms of that which is beyond all dualities. We can *sense* it although we cannot *name* it. At least this is the possibility I am inviting the reader to consider.

Some may feel that the enthusiasm for things oriental is yet another attempt to find easy solutions to the contemporary problems of western religion, as though Hinduism, Buddhism and Zen could be applied like sticking plasters to the running sores of Christianity. This would be absurd. In any case the oriental religions have problems of their own some of which resemble those of Christianity. The stifling effects of clericalism, blind acceptance of dogma and the killing of the spirit by the letter appear wherever there are human beings. Needless to say, practitioners of Zen are not exempt. Obsession with sitting meditation (zazen) and the chanting of sutras out of dreary duty are simply Zen equivalents of dutiful churchianity. R.H. Blyth has an essay somewhere called 'No more Japanese Zen thank you' in which he attacks ecclesiastical Zen. Yet there is a sense in which Christianity, for example, is able to have a greater sense of its own destiny when it sees itself through eastern eyes. Many contemporary expressions of Christianity, it seems to me, buy their modernity by sacrificing their genuinely religious content. Christianity needs to be freed from its capitulation to the common sense of the west if it is to rediscover its mysteries.

Some remarks by Heinrich Zimmer, the great scholar of the eastern traditions, supply the best perspective I can think of for seeing the present study in the broadest context. Zimmer's comments were made in lectures at Columbia University in 1942 and sound remarkably contemporary some forty years later:

> We of the Occident are about to arrive at a cross-roads that was reached by the thinkers of India some seven hundred years before Christ.... Just as in the period of the deflation of the revealed gods of the Vedic pantheon, so today revealed Christianity has been devaluated.... The philosophical dialogues of the Upanishads indicate that during the eighth century B.C. a critical shift of weight from the outer universe and tangible spheres of the body to the inner and the intangible was carrying the dangerous implications of this direction of the mind to their logical conclusion.... This we recognize as precisely the non-theistic, anthropocentric position that we ourselves are on the point of reaching today in the West, if indeed we are not already there. For where dwell the gods to whom we can uplift our hands, send forth our prayers, and make oblation? Beyond the Milky Way are only island universes, galaxy beyond galaxy in the infinitudes of space – no realm of angels, no heavenly mansions, no chairs of the blessed surrounding a diving throne of the Father, revolving in beatific consciousness about the axial mystery of the Trinity. Is there any region left in all these great reaches where the soul on its quest might expect to arrive at the feet of God, having become divested of its own material coil? Or must we not now turn rather inward, seek the divine internally, in the deepest vault, beneath the floor; hearken within

for the secret voice that is both commanding and consoling; draw from inside the grace which passeth all understanding?[15]

But, Zimmer warns, we cannot simply borrow the Indian solution;

We must enter the new period our own way and solve its questions for ourselves, because though truth, the radiance of reality, is universally one and the same, it is mirrored variously according to the mediums in which it is reflected....

Concepts and words are symbols, just as visions, rituals, and images are; so too are the manners and customs of daily life. Through all of these a transcendent reality is mirrored. They are so many metaphors reflecting and implying something which, though thus variously expressed, is ineffable, though thus rendered multiform, remains inscrutable. Symbols hold the mind to truth but are not themselves the truth, hence it is delusory to borrow them. Each civilization, every age, must bring forth its own.... We cannot borrow God. We must effect His new incarnation from within ourselves. Divinity must descend, somehow, into the matter of our own existence and participate in this peculiar life-process.'[16]

If these words sound reductionist it is because we have such a poor image of ourselves as egos in bags of skin. Such a conventional understanding of the self cannot bear the weight of the incarnation which Zimmer speaks about. The thinkers discussed in the following chapters have understood this in a very radical way. They are modern pioneers of inner space and among the most reliable, imaginative guides for those who are, in Zimmer's words, at the crossroads.

1 The new religious consciousness

THE OLD CONSCIOUSNESS

THE TIME IS EARLY evening in midsummer. The place is a soccer stadium in Birmingham, England. Forty thousand people wait to hear the evangelist's words. I sit high in the stand and scan the futuristic skyline of the city and west midlands. Motor vehicles speed into a science fiction vista of tiered roads known as spaghetti junction. Television cameras pan the scene for relaying across the Atlantic. The crowds locked outside watch the proceedings on a huge video screen. From time to time an aeroplane glides overhead. We are in the late twentieth century, 1984. No doubt about it. But why are we huddled together in this place and in need of the preacher's message? The evangelist knew why. There was once a Hebrew God – and from here I paraphrase – who created our primal ancestors and made the fruit of a certain tree strictly taboo. Adam and Eve could resist anything but temptation and plunged the human race into a form of live-now-pay-later known as sin. Meanwhile, back in the stadium, forty thousand people are wondering if there is any good news. Not to fret. There is a remedy; faith in Jesus Christ. The consequences for anyone refusing the offer could be dire. I began to muse whether by now the Buddha or Lao tzu had accepted Jesus Christ as their personal saviour or were rotting in the dungeons of heaven. It then occurred to me that I had been quite mistaken in something I had assumed to be true for a long time. I had often used the image of Aldous Huxley's Brave New World when discussing the future of religion. In

such a world, where the values of calculation and transient
sensations were all-pervasive, there could be no religion. But
of course there could be. I was listening to such a religion. A
one dimensional religion could easily survive in a one dimensional society. The industrialized setting of the evangelist's
sermon was in an ironic way a literal fulfillment of the
promise to the mythological Adam that man would have
dominion. At first it seemed to me, sitting there in the
stadium, that there was a yawning chasm between the
modernity of the scene and the antiquity of the preacher's
message. But on second thoughts they belonged together. The
evangelist was rehearsing a literalized historical version of the
myth which subdued the earth and produced the secular city
in the centre of which he stood. He spoke a horizontal
message in a horizontal culture.

The theologian Paul Tillich, speaking at the fortieth
anniversary celebration of *Time* magazine, gave a very
trenchant statement of what I have in mind here; '. . . our
culture is one-dimensional, determined by the drive toward
expansion in the horizontal line: be it the push into outer
space, be it the production of ever new and improved tools,
be it the increase in means and materials of communication,
be it the growing number of human beings to whom cultural
'goods' are available – all this is one-dimensional horizontal
expansion.'[17] Tillich went on to warn that where religion is
conceived only in a horizontal way it becomes merely
another, albeit the oldest, cultural good.

A few days after hearing the evangelist I was having my
hair cut by a teenage girl in the same city and realized in
conversation that we had both attended the same event. I
asked her what she thought of the address. She was not
impressed. I asked why. The nine words she used in reply
were as succinct as anything out of Bertrand Russell; 'He was
saying things a modern person can't accept.' No dumb
blonde, this young woman. She hadn't left her mind at the
turnstile and could spot an impossible religion when she saw
one. She knew that no adult mind now would look into

Genesis to find a literal version of the origin of the world and the entry of sin through the act of a primal couple. It may be true that evangelical forms of religion have attracted great numbers in recent years. It is equally true, however, that many thoughtful hairstylists find such a religion egotistical and embarrassing. In its more strident and fundamentalist forms it is barbaric. Sadly, such barbarism is now well and truly part of the pornography of everyday religion, whether it be the dynamite and harikari Muslim varieties or the lounge suit and T shirt Christian type which cooly consigns three quarters of the earth's population to hell or extinction.

SO WHAT'S NEW?

Not all forms of Christianity are versions of the higher lunacy. There are more profound versions available to those who have the patience to search them out. Christianity does have forgotten secrets. Yet I would say that on the faces of many Christians I have known there are deep signs of restlessness. Something fundamental has been lost and they would dearly love to discover it. There is a black hole in the soul of the modern Christian. He or she may try to hold on heroically to what the Christian beliefs are about, but it is often precisely an experience *about* something they do not possess. Faith is experienced as alienation. The American theologian William Hamilton pointed to a new phenomenon, the alienated theologian – alienated from God, Christendom, Christianity and the church. Hamilton called the theologian a Thursday's child, an agonized figure who has far to go. He was writing at the height of the death of God controversy in the mid sixties[18] but the description still has an authentic ring about it. A century before in Dover Beach, Matthew Arnold had written some very prophetic words about the tortured believer watching the sea of faith at its twentieth century ebb tide and listening to its 'melancholy, long, withdrawing roar.' I shall say more later about the faith which has ebbed but a few comments here may help the reader to see the general direction of the discussion.

There is something at the heart of Christianity in its traditional form which makes faith a potentially alienating experience in any age and not just this century. In most versions of Christianity – not merely those of crude evangelism – Jesus is presented as a religious freak. This is a strikingly consistent theme from the most conservative through to the most radical types of Christianity. In the development of theology the person of Jesus has been reverenced to a degree which has created an impossible dilemma for the Christian. The theological process of pedestalizing Jesus, from the very earliest times, has made his state of consciousness inaccessible to mere mortals. Christians are urged to follow a man who had an impossible advantage. The very thought of having the same consciousness as Jesus is doctrinally taboo. There is only one true son and the world is an orphanage. It is difficult to see how this could ever be thought to be good news. Where people have claimed to have the mind of Christ in mystical experiences they have met with suspicion and persecution.

Having said this, and acknowledging the decline of institutionalized religion in the west, in the past thirty years there has been a radical change in the religious scene. Some people have spoken of the appearance of the new mysticism. Others have called it the dawning of a new religious consciousness.[19] One of the main purposes of this book is to highlight what this movement has to say to us in the west. The great cracks which have appeared in many forms of western religion can be experienced in either of two ways. They can be seen as clear signs as the beginning of the end for ancient edifices which are about to crumble for good. On the other hand they can equally well be experienced as cracks in a hard shell which is at last unable to withstand the force of the new life trying to break free. I would myself favour the second view.

The new mysticism has broken through old barriers in a bewildering variety of fields, not merely in the religious spheres. Marilyn Ferguson, using the imagery favoured by

Theodore Roszak, has called the movement as a whole the Aquarian conspiracy in her book on personal and social transformation in the 1980s.[20] To adopt Tillich's terms again; the mystical cannot be confined to horizontal religion. The 'vertical line is effective in every creative work, in artistic as well as scientific, in ethical as well as political, in technical as well as in economic creations, and even in the power of playing.'[21] There have, of course, been developments which can more easily be identified with ancient and mystical phenomena – Buddhism, Vedanta, Zen, yoga, meditation.[22] Like any other movement, the new mysticism has had its superficial side. The tribal revolution of the young, for example, often expressed itself in YMCA Hinduism, joss stick Buddhism and Beatnik Zen to become as ephemeral as the angry young milk bar messiahs of the fifties and the Carnaby Street Marxists of the sixties. Nevertheless, all was not candyfloss. The writings of R.H. Blyth, D.T. Suzuki and Alan Watts introduced millions to very solid versions of oriental teaching. To many readers the standard western brands of religion seemed weak tea by comparison. The various forms of the new mystical movements offered a transformation of consciousness and not merely exotic things to believe. They were quite outside the well worn ruts of organized religion which, unless you have a taste for it, can have a claustrophobia all of its own. During these same decades the biblical, political image of God as the ruler of the universe was in its death throes. I remember a fellow theological student confessing to me by night, 'I'm so relieved that I don't have to believe in God anymore.' God's dead; let's have a drink.

The void in modern Christian experience was obviously one of the factors in the west's absorption of oriental ways of thinking. The emptier we are the more easily are we able to receive the unfamiliar. In the past three decades the western world was clearly empty enough to help itself to eastern wisdom. There is no doubt whatsoever that countless thousands of people have had their lives changed either through reading the likes of Blyth, Suzuki and Watts or through groups practising meditation, yoga and so on. Nevertheless, it is still true to say that millions of people involved in traditional forms of western religion have not the faintest idea of the mystical ferment of these decades. If the reader is such a person I hope that the remainder of this chapter will spell out some of the ideas which are central to this ferment. I hope too that it will provide a general context for some of the more detailed discussions of the later chapters.

DON'T SEEK AND YOU SHALL FIND

By contrast with the Thursday's child, doubt-racked theist, many of the experiences arising out of the new mystical movements have a self-authenticating quality which can take both passionate and serene forms. For those completely unfamilar with the subject I shall suggest an image of the self which may be helpful here. The commonsense of the western world tells us that we are somehow moving through time as a truck moves along a railway track. It is as though someone dropped us on a conveyor belt when we were born. If we happen to believe in the idea of progress too, it would be as though we had been dropped on to an escalator. This view of the self fits in very well with the horizontal, one dimensional outlook of which Tillich was so critical. In place of the horizontal moving image put the self as the centre of a circle. The image of the circle or wheel is a recurring one in the descriptions of transformed states of consciousness. There are many accounts but I will mention just one here, that of John Lilly, a one time resident teacher at Esalen Institute in California. He produced an autobiography of 'Inner Space' called *The Centre of the Cyclone*. Lilly explains his use of the image:

> The centre of the cyclone is that rising quiet central low-pressure place in which one can learn

to live eternally. Just outside this centre is the rotating storm of one's own ego, competing with other egos in a furious high-velocity circular dance. As one leaves the centre, the roar of the rotating wind deafens one more and more. . . . One's centred thinking-feeling-being, one's own Satoris, are in the centre only, not outside. One's pushed-pulled driven states, one's anti-Satori modes of functioning, one's self-created hells, are outside the centre. In the centre of the cyclone one is off the wheel of Karma, of life, rising to join the Creators of the Universe, the Creators of us.[23]

John Lilly admits that he found blind alleys in his spiritual progress but is fundamentally confident about his deepest experiences:

I feel here that I am a teacher, a different kind of teacher from those you have had in school, in college. . . . I am a different kind of teacher because I have 'been there.' I haven't got it from books. . . . It comes straight from inside me and I do not feel compelled to teach what I know.[24]

The same kind of atmosphere pervades Thaddeus Golas' widely read book *The Lazy Man's Guide to Enlightenment*: 'There is a paradise in and around you right now, and to be there you don't have to make a move, not even lifting your eyes from this page. You can open yourself to the diamond like perfection of everything you see and feel.'[25] I shall have more to say specifically about this kind of experience in later chapters. A large proportion of the book discusses Alan Watts' expression of the centre of the cyclone experience, to use Lilly's terms. Writing just before his death in 1973 Watts admitted that what he had been trying to express for thirty five years had met an audience reluctant to understand, as if it were too good to be true. He went on to say the following which is a perfect summary of his basic philosophy. If the reader is unfamiliar with Watts' teaching it will provide them with the clearest first statement of his philosophy that I know of. All his detailed studies can be read in the light of it:

> The point, with which Krishnamurti and the ancient Chinese Zen masters also agree, is that there is no progressive method by which the liberated and awakened state (moksha) can be attained. This state of being and consciousness has innumerable names – mystical experience, enlightenment, self-realization, cosmic consciousness, union with God, not to mention Sanskrit, Chinese, and Arabic equivalents – but none of them are satisfactory because it is altogether beyond words. Striving after this state blocks the understanding that it is already present, as does also a kind of purposive not-striving.... Memories of the past and anticipations of the future exist only now, and thus to *try* to live completely in the present is to strive for what already the case.... The same principle applies to striving for nirvana or union with God by means of so-called spiritual exercises. There is no actual necessity for a road or obstacle course to that which IS.... Beyond words, in the silencing of thought, we are already there.[26]

We may be tempted to reply that if it is pointless to try to attain what cannot be attained why try to speak about the ineffable? There is nothing wrong with using words so long as we do not think that we catch the experience in our word nets and pin it down. All vocal mystics speak in asymptotic terms, to adopt a metaphor Watts frequently used. They are, in other words, drawing a curve which is always approaching the base line but touches it only at infinity.

Like Alan Watts, Krishnamurti is also a leading figure in the new consciousness movement. His writings are discussed in the next chapter. Krishnamurti was once asked the question raised in the last paragraph. During a conversation with Krishnamurti Gerald Heard learned that the philosopher was about to embark on a lecture tour in Australia. Heard asked why he bothered to do so much talking and thinking if he wanted to free people from such things. Krishnamurti's talks inevitably attracted followers which seemed to be self-defeating in Heard's view. Krishnamurti's reply is intriguing. Imagine, he said, someone having business in the city and calling in the lecture hall merely to shelter from the rain. They could – possibly – see the point of Krishnamurti's address without *seeking* enlightenment. In the writings of the new mystical movements there is a great deal of talk about a quest or search for spiritual understanding and enlightenment. However, we have to stress the point made by two of the chief figures in this study that the human mind cannot search for and find enlightenment. Krishnamurti in particular constantly warns that the human mind always finds what it seeks. That's its problem. Stephen Levine puts it very well; 'No one who wants to be enlightened will ever be enlightened because what we are enlightened *from* is that someone wishing to be enlightened. Wishing to be enlightened is like the ego wanting to be present at its own funeral.'[27] Search, then, is an ambiguous word. As Levine comments again; 'One of the things that blocks us from whatever this enlightenment might be is our hunger for what we imagine en-light-enment to be. Enlightenment can become our greatest cause of suffering, because it's our greatest longing. It's our greatest 'being elsewhere.'[28] If the ego is an abstraction, an illusion, then clearly the ego cannot seek. It cannot *do* anything about it and it cannot *not* do anything about it. The ego cannot get rid of a non-existent ego. The experience is neither easy nor difficult to attain. If it is easy, it must be easy for someone. If it is difficult, it must be difficult for someone. Nevertheless, the ego feeling may well disappear if a person acts completely consistently on the assumption that they are an ego, just as a fool, says Blake, who persists in his folly will become wise.

The breakthrough comes when something genuinely un-

known comes into our lives, something which we are not projecting; not by *solving* the mystery but by *becoming* the
mystery. This is the point of the Sufi saying; God is not found
by seeking, and never found by those who don't seek. The
seeker is the ego and the seeker disappears through the
seeking. Here is a Zen story:

> A hen-pecked man watches his wife dying and
> feels that his freedom is not far away. However,
> she knows what he is thinking and warns him not
> to feel too happy. 'When I die I will become a
> ghost and haunt you and nag your thoughts.'
>
> She dies, keeps reappearing and reads his inten-
> tions and sexual desires. In despair he visits a Zen
> master with his problem. The master gives him a
> bag of pebbles and says; 'Your wife is a projection.
> Nevertheless, if she appears again ask her how
> many pebbles are in the bag. If she can tell you the
> right number count them immediately and come
> to me. If she cannot tell you come and tell me just
> the same.'
>
> The man returned home and his wife was
> waiting. 'I know where you have been – to see that
> phoney Zen master and he has given you a bag of
> pebbles...' and so on.
>
> The man is at the end of his sanity and shouts
> 'Okay! You tell me how many!'
>
> Immediately, she disappeared.

The Zen master was using an upaya or skilful means to bring
about the realization that his wife's appearance was an
illusion. Because the man himself did not know the number he
could not project it. It was a genuinely unknown.

The nature of the self is the central issue which marks the
difference between the old and the new religious consciousness. For many, traditional religion stinks of the ego. It offers
us models to imitate which inflate – or cripple – the ego. It
modifies rather than transforms our consciousness. It does

not free us in a radical way from the known, conventional self to use Krishnamurti's terms. I shall say more in chapter six about how Christianity may appear when freed from its traditional shell but it may be useful to make a few observations here as signs of things to come. I referred earlier to an inherent impossibility at the heart of the Christian message as conventionally conceived. We are urged to follow a man whose state of consciousness has become inaccessible to us. But it may be that we can begin to regard this very impossibility in a new way. The teachings of Jesus can be taken in the same spirit as the Zen master in the pebble bag story; seriously try to do what he says – and fail. The illusory nature of the ego may appear when we try to do what the ego cannot do by its very nature. The sayings of Jesus can be seen in a new light. They become double binds to adopt Gregory Bateson's term. 'You *shall* love . . . .' 'You *must* be born again . . . .' 'You are my friends if . . . .' These are demands to *do* what can only *happen*. The demand for spontaneous love is no less oppressive than the demands of the Jewish law. How could anyone, for example, be natural on purpose? When we see the absurdity of such things the 'Thou *shalts*' of Jesus can be seen as thought-stoppers and perform the same function as koans in Zen Buddhism. The I who is asked the koan – or who tries to meet the demand – is not the same *I* who solves the koan or meets the demand.

THE FUTURE ISN'T WHAT IT USED TO BE

In the last few pages I have attempted to underline in a very simple way something which is central to the thinkers we are about to discuss. If there is a search, it is a journey to where we are. The place is *here*. Now I shall spell out another major theme; the reality of the present and the illusion of time. The time is *now*. We are never given three moments – the past, present and the future. At any point in our lives our consciousness has a quality of nowness about it. It is always now.

Another Zen story:

> A Zen monk was sentenced to death by a ruler
> who then declared, 'You have only twenty four
> hours – how are you going to live them?'
>
> The monk laughed and said, 'Moment to
> moment – as I have always lived! There has never
> been anything more than this moment for me.
> What does it matter whether I have twenty four
> hours or twenty four years? I have always lived in
> this moment so one moment is more than enough
> for me. Twenty four hours is too much – one
> moment is quite enough.'

The past and future are the abstract borders of an eternal
present. To think that we actually ever live through a past or
a future is like thinking that we live in the walls of a room.
We live in the space. We are deceived into thinking that the
abstract borders are the real in the same way that an audience
is deceived by the magician's patter. We are the victims of
'misdirection' to borrow an image used by Jacob Needleman;
'Misdirection is the art of attracting someone's attention so
that he looks where you want him to look and, as a result,
sees what you want him to see.'[29] Our consciousness often
appears to comprise a very real past preserved in memory and
a real future which we can, hopefully, expect to experience.
Both appear real. Our sense of the present, in fact, seems an
abstraction. It is only too well symbolized by the second
finger on a watch. It is a hairline. The present seems to go
before it arrives. We feel we have no time. We have a past
and a future but merely a split-second abstract present. In
reality, the reverse is the case. Take a coin for example. The
front and back are geometrical abstractions, like the 'ends' of
a stick. Similarly, the past and future are abstractions. The
reality is the coin itself, the stick, the present. Not to see this
is, I would say, to miss the heart of that to which religion
points. Conventional wisdom tells us that the gloomiest thing
we could say of someone's life is that it has no future. On the

contrary, the true poverty is not to have a present; not living but hoping to live.

It would be absurd to say that no one has ever said this before. It is found in all kinds of mystical writings. I am absolutely sure too that millions of nameless people who would never call themselves mystics have a sense of the immediacy of the present which is the supreme reality in their lives. I have no doubt about that. From within the Christian tradition, in *Self-Abandonment to Divine Providence*, Jean-Pierre de Caussade writes; 'The present moment is always full of infinite treasure, it contains far more than you have the capacity to hold. Faith is the measure; what you find in the present moment will be according to the measure of your faith.' Nevertheless, it is still true, I believe, that such a statement is the exception in Christianity. In that tradition life seems interesting only historically. The importance of the present depends on its place in a causal chain; what came before it and what it will lead to. I shall pick up this vital issue in later chapters.

LOST CHRISTIANITY

The appearance of the mystical movements of the past few decades has taken place largely outside of the mainstream western religious traditions. These movements have reminded us of something blindingly obvious which, it seems, we too rarely sense. This is, as I have said, that our place is *here* and our time is *now*. In its obsession with history Christianity has lost its hereness and nowness. In 1980 Jacob Needleman produced a study, *Lost Christianity*,[30] which discussed the question of whether there is a lost holy state of consciousness for which Christians yearn. Needleman found signs of a lost tradition but admits in another book that he had often felt 'that the only secrets left in Christianity were yet more words and thoughts.'[31] Many other people have felt the same. Yet, despite the wordy and ossified churches, people do discover

in themselves just such a holy state of consciousness in
unlikely places and at unlikely times. Satoris are as likely in
the streets as anywhere else. To use less fashionable language,
we can learn about Being in the backyard. Thomas Merton
was courageous enough to use such a western philosophical
term to express the nature of Zen. He called it 'the ontological
awareness of pure being beyond subject and object, an immediate grasp of being in its "suchness" and "thusness." '32 I
would agree. Merton is talking about a self-authenticating
experience of the sheer wonder and existence of the world.
This is a form of forbidden knowledge in contrast to the conventional consensus which is standard in formal education. I
have long thought about how such forbidden knowledge
could be related to the public forms of Christianity. If the lost
Christianity is to be found it is, I think, in the pursuit of such
a task. Such a version of Christianity will be surprisingly
different from the one we easily recognize. The lost
Christianity to be recovered is not a pristine version of
historical Christianity. It is something *we* have lost. It will be
the remembering of something we have always known in our
deepest selves. Through a shift in consciousness we recognize
(re-cognize) what was always there.

One of the major elements which could help Christianity to
evoke its lost secrets is its contact with the orient. It is well
known that no less a figure than C.G. Jung, in his commentary on *The Secret of the Golden Flower*, warns the westerner
of the dangers of trying to ape oriental ways of thinking. Yet
in another place he observes; 'It seems quite true that the East
is at bottom of the spiritual changes we are passing through
today. Only this East is not a Tibetan monastery full of
mahatmas but, in a sense, lies within us.'33

Some writers have suggested that we should not think that
the stream of wisdom flows only one way, from east to west.
The great mythologist Joseph Campbell has commented that
'the wise men westward of Iran have partaken of the fruit of
the knowledge of good and evil, whereas those on the other
side of that cultural divide, in India and the Far East, have

relished only the fruit of eternal life. However, the two links
... come together in the center of the garden, where they
form a single tree at the base, branching out when they reach
a certain height. Likewise, the two mythologies spring from
the base in the Near East. And if man should taste of both
fruits he would become, we have been told, as God himself
(Genesis 3.22) – which is the boon that the meeting of East
and West today is offering to us all.'[34] This present study is a
small gesture which hopefully points an encouraging hand to
the common root of these vast and rich traditions.

TO SEEK THE ASS YOU ARE RIDING ON

This is an old Chinese proverb which encapsulates much that
I would like to say. What would it be like to find the ass?
Countless people ask this question in their own particular
way. Alan Watts once received a letter from a fifteen year old
girl which read something like this; 'Dear Mr. Watts, Are you
enlightened? If you are, I would like you to help me because I
would like to be enlightened too.' I have no idea what Alan
Watts said in reply, although I could hazard a guess. D.T.
Suzuki, the great interpreter of Zen to the west, was asked
what it was like to be enlightened. He replied that it was just
like ordinary living only a few inches above the ground. Enlightenment undoubtedly has to do with the dawning of light
but it also carries the sense of being light rather than heavy or
grave. The enlightened have a stillness in themselves at the
deepest level. They transcend the swirling movement of the
rat race. In the words of one of John Lennon's songs they
watch the wheels go round:

> I'm just sitting here watching the wheels go round
> and round. . . .
> No longer riding on the merry go round I just had
> to let it go.

As I suggested earlier, in discussions with people completely unfamiliar with the subject I have found the image of the wheel of consciousness particularly helpful. This makes the point in a similar way to John Lilly's image of the cyclone. On the wheel of consciousness there are those far out on the circumference who are completely taken in by the conventions of thought and action. They are enrolled. People are progressively less hypnotized the closer they are to the centre. The enlightened are the still point of the turning world. They are on the spindle which pins down the wheel. They are off the wheel of karma. The Tibetan wheel of life is a particularly suggestive image. The wheel is divided into six segments and occupied by creatures in various stages of attachment – including the divine realm. The way off the wheel is either through the centre or through the heart of the particular form of attachment in each realm.

The enlightened one may return to the wheel while retaining the centred state of consciousness. They may live, that is, on two levels. At one level, the absolute level, they are at peace knowing that the universe cannot make a mistake – all is Tao. This encompasses all relativities and polarities. The second level is the everyday involved life of distinctions between good and evil, self and other, the knower and the known. There is, for example, an obvious difference between up and down at the relative level in a room. The same distinction would be meaningless in the larger context of outer space.

We are dealing therefore with qualities of consciousness. As Golas comments in *The Lazy Man's Guide*, 'Everything that happens on earth can be experienced on any of thousands of different vibration levels, from the most euphoric to the gloomiest. We are entirely free to emphasize any level we wish.' The majority of theologians and philosophers in the west seem to be on quite a different vibration level from those immersed in the western oriental movements. This book tries to help the former to feel the 'vibes' and to allow a little Zen to fall. As R.H. Blyth reminds us, 'To teach Zen means to unteach; to see life steadily and see it whole, the answer not being divided from the question.'[35]

2 The unremembered moment

ONE OF THE MOST obvious tensions between the philosophi-. cal establishment and the approach I want to discuss is that concerning the status and function of language. Does language reveal or conceal the truth? Some comments by Aldous Huxley in his book *The Doors of Perception* put the dilemma as succinctly as one could wish to have it. In the early sections of the book he considers the view that the function of the brain and nervous system is eliminative rather than productive. They reduce our awareness and increase our chances of survival at the same time. Our narrowed attention helps to us notice what is edible and what is dangerous; but at a cost. Reduced awareness is in turn given expression through language-systems and implicit philosophies. Huxley then makes the following comment:

> Every individual is at once the beneficiary and the victim of the linguistic tradition into which he or she has been born – the beneficiary inasmuch as language gives access to the accumulated records of other people's experience, the victim in so far as it confirms him in the belief that reduced aware-ness is the only awareness and as it bedevils his sense of reality, so that he is all too apt to take his concepts for data, his words for actual things.[36]

In the course of this study I shall follow up the implications of this distinction between the functions of language. Despite the current disagreements between Wittgenstein's followers and empirically minded philosophers, it is true to say that most philosophers of religion have attempted to pay more attention to the role language plays in the lives of the people who use it. We are perhaps a little more aware – to use both Wittgenstein's and Huxley's terms – of the depth grammar of the accumulated records of experience. Yet if Huxley's comments have any truth in them even sympathetic attention to deep meanings in the language may amount to no more than a sophisticated attachment to our own reduced awareness. We are simply becoming more familiar with the contents of our semantic prisons, to use another of Huxley's terms.

Our assessment of the role of language in religion is obviously crucial. As I indicated earlier, this book is mainly concerned with the kind of religious experience described in the works of Alan Watts and, to a lesser degree, in those of Krishnamurti. Running through both philosophers' thought is the conviction that language is somehow a veil over reality. They both make very radical attempts to show that language makes human beings the victims of reduced awareness. To bring out the full force of Watts' approach I have chosen to discuss also a philosophical view which seems, at first sight, to be a quite contrary position. This view, based mainly on the thought of Ludwig Wittgenstein, develops the sense in which man is the beneficiary of language. In this second approach it makes no sense to draw a distinction between language itself and that which it inadequately represents. I shall hopefully spell this out in more detail later and merely state it baldly here to hint at a wider context for what follows. A modern Wittgensteinian, D.Z.Phillips, acknowledges, for example, that there can be inadequate uses of language 'but it makes no sense to say that language itself is inadequate.'[37] Thus, in the case of religion, the reality of God, divinity, and so on, is to be found in the language itself. The language is not *about* something independent of itself.

The two different approaches to language have been crudely summarized here. The chapters which follow attempt to draw out this distinction a little more subtly. It is a distinction which appears again and again in different guises in many of the issues that arise about religion.

KRISHNAMURTI: WHAT MORE DO YOU WANT?

I have chosen to open this discussion with the teachings of Krishnamurti for two reasons. He offers a radical, no-non-sense statement of the view that sees us as the victims of language. Secondly, his work provides a fruitful introduction to an approach developed more colourfully and positively by Alan Watts.

Many readers may be unfamiliar with Krishnamurti's writings and may be helped by having here two brief quotations which convey the flavour of his approach to religion and philosophy. Some years ago, during an encounter with Aldous and Laura Huxley, Krishnamurti was asked to define a religious person. Part of his answer was as follows:

> A religious man is a man who is alone – not lonely, you understand, but alone – with no theories or dogmas, no opinion, no background ...free of conditioning...to be a religious man, one must destroy everything – destroy the past, destroy one's convictions, interpretations, deceptions – destroy *all* self-hypnosis-destroy until there is no center; you understand, *no* center.[38]

We may feel that Krishnamurti is espousing the view of one particular eastern tradition. This would be to misunderstand him. It is very clear from his published teachings that all religious and philosophical traditions are subjected to this censure. Traditions, of whatever kind, too easily become a barrier between us and reality. At one point in his *Commentaries on Living* he puts the matter very succinctly:

> We are distracted by words, by symbols; we rarely feel except through the stimulation of the term, the description. The word 'God' is not God, but that word leads us to react according to our conditioning. We can find out the truth or the falseness of God only when the word 'God' no longer creates in us certain habitual or physiological responses.[39]

These comments are bound to sound bewildering to some people. How are we then, they may ask, to remain steadfast in the faith? Krishnamurti's statements often sound quite contrary to the way religion is usually discussed. We may be less disorientated and more easily grasp the essence of his view by glancing briefly at some recent findings in the psychology of consciousness. Jerome Bruner, for example, has concentrated on the way in which what we innocently call 'ordinary awareness' is, in fact, a construction. Robert Ornstein summarises Bruner's view in the following way:

> As we mature, we attempt to make more and more consistent 'sense' out of the mass of information arriving at our receptors. We develop stereotyped systems, or *categories*, for sorting input. The set of categories we develop is limited, much more limited than the input...what we actually experience...is the *category* which is evoked by a particular stimulus, *not* the occurrence in the external world.[40]

We may, for example, categorize someone as 'aggressive' and subsequently assimilate anything they do in terms of this category. In psychological jargon this is 'habituation,' our 'orienting reaction' to new experiences. Faced with new stimulus we cope by categorizing it. We register it in terms of a set category. It then ceases to be 'new.' It is out of our awareness and on 'automatic.' Krishnamurti is making similar assertions about our total experience of the world. Could it be that what we call the real world is, in fact, a collective projection which we have learned through habit and passed on to every new generation as the sober truth? Krishnamurti argues that this is the case and that the habit can be broken. Release from the grip comes through a mode of consciousness or awareness expressed by Krishnamurti in different ways as a state of continuous meditation. This is not, as one would expect from him, something that must be done for a purpose, something one had to achieve.

Other people, of course, have given the same diagnosis of our condition as Krishnamurti does but have advocated different remedies. The whole chemical mysticism movement, for example, linked with Timothy Leary, is based on the conviction that our selective apparatus, which provides the stereotypes, may be suspended by the controlled use of psychic vitamins. A mind set free from the habitual categories may experience sense impressions in new and perhaps startling patterns. Krishnamurti would probably regard this solution as itself an expression of the malady it seeks to cure. Drugs, no less than ideologies and habitual religion, are the offer of yet another trip on borrowed wings.

To adopt the psychological terms for the moment, Krishnamurti is saying that what most people experience for most of the time is a 'category' rather than reality as it is. To experience life only within such stereotyped systems is not to be alive at all in the sense that matters. It follows that any world-view, religion, belief or doctrine may be instrumental in putting us on 'automatic.' They become barriers to the real. Yet Krishnamurti is attacking much more than mere dogma. His central target is thought itself. He raises what he calls the 'impossible question'; can the mind empty itself of the known?

Reading Krishnamurti can be a disorientating experience. His teachings are well clear of the much worn tramlines of a great deal of moral and religious thought. His name does not appear in technical philosophical discussions and rarely in theological books. Nevertheless, he appears to have a wide lay following if book sales are a reliable guide. Could it be that he is a hack? Hardly. The most likely reason for his absence from philosophical and religious debates is that he does not fit into the standard classifications. If his teachings are true, of course, they undermine the normal, common-sense assumptions underlying many of the debates. His talks and writings are directed towards evoking an experience which eludes the word games of philosophers and theologians. This is his intention, at least, so far as I can see.

Krishnamurti has published no systematic account of his own thought. He would probably laugh at the idea. Most of his published writings are either verbatim reports of dialogues with groups or his own records of meetings with individuals who came to talk over a problem. As I have already suggested, there is no attempt on his part to take up detailed points in discussions of the kind found in religious or philosophical journals. Many of the usual concepts and categories which are normally found in the latter are often only mentioned by Krishnamurti to be dismissed or treated in a quite unusual way. Nevertheless, anyone unfamiliar with his thought is bound to begin by asking the questions implicit in the more orthodox analyses; Is there a God?, What is it to believe in something?, What is knowledge?

It is worth noting in passing the strange circumstances of Krishnamurti's childhood. He had been found roaming the beaches of India and adopted by the Theosophical Society to be prepared for his role as world teacher, Messiah, Maitreya, the Buddha-to-come. The Order of the Star in the East was created for this purpose. Mary and Emily Lutyens have recorded the extraordinary events in the first forty years of Krishnamurti's life, culminating in his rejection of the role.[41] He dissolved the Order of the Star in 1929 with the statement that his only concern was to set men absolutely, unconditionally free:

> I maintain that Truth is a pathless land, and you
> cannot approach it by any path whatsoever, by
> any religion, by any sect.

These words accurately reflect the nature of his teaching since then. His disaffection with the Theosophical Society and its beliefs caused great pain to his close friends at first. In a letter of April 1932 to Emily Lutyens, he wrote; 'If you are alert, free from ideas, beliefs, etc. in the present, then you perceive infinitely and this perception is joy.'[42] Mary Lutyens comments that Emily was more confused than ever. Krishnamurti himself simply asked, 'What more do you want?' We are not told Emily's reply but, no doubt,many would have said, 'Much more!' I mention this small incident because it reveals the spirit of Krishnamurti's teachings throughout the following fifty years. Just why do we want to know whether there is a God? Why do we want to know of a method which will liberate us? Just what is lacking from our experience now of the eternal present? The philosophically inclined would want to know, of course, what it *means* to perceive infinitely. The religiously minded would want to know what sort of an experience it could be. These questions will be taken up later. We need to remember at the outset, however, that Krishnamurti is unwilling himself to play the role of guru or religious hero. He has no good word to say of either species. Nor does he offer his own teaching as a means of liberation; 'We are not professing a new theory, a new philosophy, nor bringing a religious revelation. There is no teacher, no saviour, no master, no authority.'[43]

It is as well to make clear the radicality of his intentions right at the start. Krishnamurti does not offer what could vaguely be called a meaning or purpose for life. If we did discover such a thing it would 'not be worth that pebble on the path.'[44] To ask for such a purpose or meaning is to escape from reality; 'you are asking for a change of prisons.'[45] At first glance such remarks sound like extreme nihilism. Krishnamurti himself would probably call it purity of thought or, rather, absence of thought. It is in observations like these that he tests the patience of some readers. What are we to make of someone who disagrees so vehemently with standard ways of thinking and yet claims to offer nothing to replace them? The most advisable course at this stage is to take it on faith that Krishnamurti is, in fact, offering a radically alternative way of interpreting experience, besides which all philosophical and religious disputes sound like childrens' squabbles. The advice he gives to anyone wishing to consider such an alternative is best put in his own words; 'Forget all you know about yourself . . . all you have ever thought about yourself.'[46]

ON BEING LATE FOR THE FEAST

The American academic drop-out turned-guru, Ram Dass, comments on a problem he used to have while trying to eat pizza.[47] Just as he was about to take a bite, he heard an inward voice say, 'Eating pizza.' Putting the activity into words detracted from the sheer enjoyment of biting into onions, mushrooms and cheese. It was as though he was paying more attention to the label or echo of the experience than to the experience itself. This seems to me to be a good example of the kind of point Krishnamurti is making. We take the lead from the known, the category, and always arrive just a little late for the feast. The great feast is, of course, the unremembered moment, life here and now, free from the clutter of so-called mental images and categories. To use a different metaphor; it is as though we were in a room walled with mirrors waiting for our reflections to take the lead. We make no new movement because we follow the image of what we have done already. We do not so much act as *re*-act.

One of the first things that readers of Krishnamurti notice is that apparently harmless words like thought, mind, self, experience have a pejorative sense for him. The mind, for example, is the real cause of our problems and he mocks the very idea of freedom of thought. Thought lacks immediacy, it is never new, and merely the response of memory, experience, knowledge.[48] This, to say the least, sounds like an attack on one of man's most cherished possessions; his power to think. Few will concede that anything has been 'understood' unless it has been translated into words and a framework of reflective thought. But this is probably one major reason for Krishnamurti's complaint that, in fact, thought cripples us. All thinking is classification and measuring.[49] Based on accumulated memories, thought creates a pattern,[50] or a net[51] and has only relative freedom within it. Thought, so defined, can never find 'what is . . . beyond its borders.[52]

How then do we escape from the mind's self-constructed prison? This is the 'impossible' question according to

Krishnamurti; 'Can the mind empty *itself* of the known?.'[53]
He never seems to give a direct answer to this question but
observes that the answer will come if the question is put with
earnestness and passion. It is certainly not something the self
or the ego could achieve. The self is an aspect of thought itself; 'I' is itself a thought. The 'me' or the imagined centre of
consciousness is essentially separative; it measures and produces fragmentation.[54] The mind then time-binds its fragmented experiences into an imaginary continuity. Hence the
self over against the world; the observer forever casting its
shadow on what it observes[55] and seeing everything in the
light of an image based on accumulated experiences. Therefore, says Krishnamurti, thought is always old and the self is
a bore.[56]

It follows from this that 'experience,' the sacred cow of
many writers on religion, is a word in the vocabulary of those
who live in the image-dominated state. For Krishnamurti experience is a synonym for inattention. Deliberately to seek
experience confirms that person in a state of illusion and
immaturity. Nevertheless, despite all that has been said, the
mind – whatever its present state of experiential and episte-
mological sin – paradoxically holds all the answers. There is
no need to read books about it, says Krishnamurti, 'Watch
your own mind, it is all there.'[57] This recalls Berdyaev's
comment that 'Man is not a fragmentary part of the world but
contains the whole riddle of the universe and the solution of
it.'[58] It needs to be said too that to live fully in the unremembered moment is not to be without what Krishnamurti calls
'technological memories' – name, address, telephone number,
and so on. To live in the eternal present is not to be a stone
buddha in some kind of catatonic trance; it is to be on time
for the feast.

TRUTH HAS NO TRADITION –
IT CANNOT BE HANDED DOWN

This sentence is a quotation from Krishnamurti's recently

published journal.[59] It is a blunt warning of what we might expect him to say about belief and knowledge. For him, beliefs, and religious beliefs in particular, are self-consoling projections based on fear.[60] To underline his view on this subject we could well reverse a common saying into 'I'll see it when I believe it.' Belief and disbelief are products of conditioning[61] and distort our view of the true and the real. His rejection of doctrines and beliefs includes a summary and wholesale rejection of Christian theology. He comments at one point that 'one must obviously discard all theologies and all beliefs.'[62] The transformed state of consciousness of which he is speaking makes such preoccupations seem a waste of time.

Belief, like thought and experience, is something which does not hamper a person who is truly alive. It is another sacred cow. So is knowledge. At first this seems harder to swallow. After all, if we can say we 'know' something we have avoided projection and speculation. Nevertheless, knowledge like thought casts its shadow; 'We know only the image or the memory.'[63] Life is always new, always in the present. Knowledge conditions our responses into concepts and categories and prevents responses which are free, ecstatic, real, true. A person who is truly aware lives every moment as a mystery but 'knowledge cannot contain mystery.'[64] Knowledge, in fact, simply informs our projection. The knowledge we have acquired through experience is imposed on what we observe. The mysterious becomes the familiar: 'You can only recognize something you have known before.'[65] In one passage he expresses the point particularly starkly; 'If you know, you are already in your grave.'[66]

What sense then is there in saying that something is true? If we cannot believe or know something is true, what meaning is left for the word? It is clear that Krishnamurti sees knowledge or belief as having nothing to do with truth. Truth is 'what is.' Belief and knowledge are too closely tied to the creations of the mind. Truth comes only through direct, immediate perception and is something which comes unbidden.[67] It follows that truth is not something to be sought. The seeker finds only what he wants to find. What then is it which cannot be believed in, known and which is nevertheless real? Could it be God?

GOD, RELIGION AND THE IDOLS CARVED BY THE MIND

Krishnamurti believes in nothing. How could he believe in God? It is true that he frequently refers to God as a projection, a comforting illusion; 'God is put in heaven by thought.'[68] It is also true that he seems to have a put-down attitude to all the subjects I have discussed so far. We have to remember, however, that, as normally understood, these are symptoms of a reduced state of awareness which comes through our reducing valves as – to use Huxley's phrase – a measly trickle. In this state of consciousness, the notion of God, like any other idea, creates in us certain habitual responses. We seek the God we 'know,' an idea. How could this be God? To believe in such a God, according to Krishnamurti, is to believe in yourself, a belief which has very little significance since it is a projection, a product of conditioning.[69]

If most of Krishnamurti's comments about the idea of God seem negative they are even more so on the subject of religion in general; 'Organized religion is the frozen thought of man.'[70] He is not thinking only of western religions; all religions are now 'utterly meaningless.'[71] He is particularly severe on tradition, ritual and sacred books which he prides himself on not having read.[72] Despite the verbal fireworks against God and religion, his views on these issues are ambiguous. He does reserve an acceptable use at times for both the idea of God and the phenomenon of religion. The religions, as accumulations of tradition, monolithic entities, and so on, may be meaningless for him, yet he can say that 'to be religious is to be sensitive to reality,'[73] and that religion 'is the feeling of sacredness, of compassion, of love.'[74] In other words, at times he uses the word religion to express what is at the heart of his own positive teaching. But what of God? This is more difficult to determine.

We know that Krishnamurti is contemptuous of God as a psychological safeguard. That much is clear. There are times when he is willing to imply that 'God' is interchangeable with love or simply with 'what is.' Take, for example, the following remark; 'When there is love, which is its own eternity, then there is no search for God, because love is God.'[75] Again; 'When there is no illusion "what is" is god or any other name that can be used. So god, or whatever name you give it, is when *you* are not.'[76] Observations like these, however, do not take us very far. We may have some understanding of what he means by love, but what can 'what is' mean? Krishnamurti would probably say at this point that we are getting ourselves into the tortuous debates about theology and belief because we have missed the essential heart of his teachings. We are puzzled about 'God' and 'what is' because we imagine these to be realities somehow separate and external to ourselves. We have identified ourselves with an idea we have of ourselves. We fail to see that the observer is the observed. There is no reason, other than blind habit, why we should separate ourselves from what we call our environment in the way we commonly do. To overcome this separation is to shatter the reducing valves. The present, unremembered moment is complete in itself. This is the nameless experience 'of which one cannot speak.' If we wish to use the exclamation 'God!' in this state of consciousness, so be it. This state closely resembles what the Hindus call *sat-chit-ananda* (reality-awareness-ecstasy). Life is ecstatic play just as it is, if only we could see it. To be in ecstasy is to stand outside, free from the standardized, set role of the self, the three dimensional illusion.

Krishnamurti's own term for this state of awareness is meditation. He is contemptuous, however, of meditation as a discipline or a form of introspection. These are simply highbrow ways of becoming more selfish. To meditate as a deliberate policy is to be involved in a self-expansive enterprise, an improving exercise, with special times and bodily postures. By contrast, Krishnamurti states that true meditation is a permanent state of awareness. Simply watch without identification, comparison and condemnation. All of the latter imply an existing standard on the basis of which we classify and choose. The truly aware do not choose; they are choicelessly aware; 'Only the person who is confused chooses.'[77] Many will find this comment itself confusing. Robert Hollings, for example, writing in his book *Transcendental Meditation* (1982), admits that Krishnamurti's philosophy is fascinating to read but that it is impossible to *do* what Krishnamurti suggests. Hollings compares reading Krishnamurti's books to learning to dive from a swimming board. We are instructed up the ladder, along the board to the very edge and then simply told to dive, without knowing how to do so or how to overcome our fear. I suspect that Krishnamurti would reply that Hollings' imagery betrays a misunderstanding about what it is to be unconditionally aware. It is not a state into which we *decide* to enter or could be instructed to enter by means of a technique.

These comments bring us to the climax of what we have said so far about Krishnamurti's teachings. All of them seem to depend on there being, in fact, the possibility of pure, unconditioned awareness. To use his own terms; 'Seeing is not analysing. In analysing there is the analyser and the analysed, a fragmentation.'[78] It is precisely on this issue that the full force of modern scepticism would be directed against Krishnamurti. Many would deny the possibility of an innocent eye. All observation is translation and interpretation. Krishnamurti would agree that human beings do indeed experience in this way in their unenlightened state but that there is a mode of awareness which is not so conditioned. This is a very basic issue and I shall take it up again after discussing the thought of Alan Watts. I have been chiefly concerned in these few pages to consider Krishnamurti's teachings as he sees them himself, without bringing in all the contentious issues which inevitably come to mind. I shall break off the discussion of his thought for the moment with a passage which summarizes much of what he is about and which, incidently, raises another question to be picked up later. This is that Krishnamurti reduces life to the point instant. Life is atomized and disintegrates. For the time being, however, let Krishnamurti have the last word;

> The important thing...is to be aware from moment to moment without accumulating the experience which awareness brings; because, the moment you accumulate, you are aware only according to that accumulation, according to that pattern, according to that experience...your awareness is conditioned by your accumulation and therefore there is no longer observation but merely translation.'[79]

THE FLY AND THE FLY-BOTTLE

More than one commentator has compared Wittgenstein with a Zen master.[80] He offers clarity and liberation. He imagines himself being asked the question 'What is your aim in philosophy?' and answers; 'To shew the fly the way out of the fly-bottle.'[81] He uses other metaphors to express the same idea. Language, Wittgenstein says, casts a spell and holds us captive. Philosophy is meant to break the spell; 'Philosophy is a battle against the bewitchment of our intelligence by means of language.'[82] I am concerned for the moment with just one of the spells that Wittgenstein breaks; that which bewitches us into assuming that language and understanding require thought. I refer to it here because it closely resembles the spell Krishnamurti wishes to break. We shall see that Wittgenstein's thought partly supports and partly contradicts Krishnamurti's approach.

The common sense view of the relation of words to thought would be something like the following. Our spoken words give expression to our thoughts. Language is the medium through which thought becomes public. Without thoughts the words would be mere noises. Without words thoughts would be locked in our private worlds. There would be no way of communicating our thoughts to others. Therefore, to understand language we require thought.

Wittgenstein shows that this way of conceiving the relation of thought to language is a picture which holds us captive. It is seductive but mistaken. Language does not require thought. For Wittgenstein, language and understanding are rooted in what he called 'practice.' In other words, we discover the meaning of language by plotting its use, not by connecting it with mental entities called 'thoughts.' If we are captivated by the notion that thoughts bring language to life, Wittgenstein suggests that we externalize our thoughts. He offers us a parable of someone being asked to fetch a red flower from a nearby meadow. How would that person know which flower to select? Imagine that we are asked to fetch a red object. According to the theory Wittgenstein is trying to combat, we have a thought of 'red' in our minds. Because of this we are able to recognize the object we were sent to collect. Now, suggests Wittgenstein, externalize the 'thought' by painting a red patch. We look at it and then fetch the object which matches the patch's colour. But it is not the patch itself which enables us to collect the correct object. Unless a person is familiar with a practice involving the word red, he will not know what to do with the patch. The painting or patch of red is vivid but superfluous. It adds nothing. The same must be true of the 'thought' red. The latter is less vivid and is as superfluous as the patch for the same reason. Neither the external image – the patch – nor the internal image – the thought – gives life to the words. Thought is not required for the understanding of language. The activity is the bedrock of language and its meaning is its use. Language can operate perfectly well and meaningfully without a single, fleeting thought. We have agreed to use language in a particular way and this involves following rules. As Wittgenstein observes;

'When I obey a rule, I do not choose. I obey the rule *blindly*.'[83] This means that I do not have to interpret my thoughts in a way which subsequently affects my actions. I simply act.

At first glance, all of this could look like a form of mindless behaviourism. Human beings could appear as slaves to language use; mere automata. People who have this impression, however, usually assume the Cartesian model of the mind: I am inside my head affecting the external world by giving instructions to my body through the medium of thoughts. On the basis of this model, to dispense with thought is the end of human beings as we know them. They would be empty shells having the semblance of life through responding to stimuli, including the sound of words. The truth is, of course, that it is exactly this model of the mind that Wittgenstein wishes to expose as an illusion. He dispenses with the little mental chauffeur in the head.

I have said enough already for us to see an obvious connection between, on the one hand, Wittgenstein's views on the relation of thought and language and Krishnamurti's teachings on activity free of thought on the other. Both philosophers would agree that all people do have thoughts. Wittgenstein is saying that they are superfluous for understanding language. Krishnamurti is saying that language and thought prevent us from realizing our true nature. Putting the two approaches together in this way raises a rather obvious question. Krishnamurti says that enlightenment comes through acting free of thought. Wittgenstein says that we act free of thoughts in any case. Does it follow that everyone is enlightened fundamentally, although many may not realise it?

Although Krishnamurti acknowledges no particular religious allegiance, his teachings on the nature of the self do closely resemble the Buddhist and Taoist views. One of the strong themes in many forms of Buddhism is that, in fact, every person at all times is in the Buddha mind but that not everyone realises that this is so. Wittgenstein's own response would probably be a refusal to speak in such terms as a philosopher. He may well have said, however, that his view of the relation of thought to language does not predispose us to reject Buddhism. Something like this has been said by Chris Gudmunsen in his analysis of the close affinities of Madhyamika Buddhism to Wittgenstein's thought; 'All modern adherents of the Madhyamika ought...to be Wittgensteinians, but the followers of Wittgenstein need not become Buddhists.'[84] Wittgenstein was combating the way a metaphysical picture of the relation of thought to language misleads us in our attempts to understand language. He does not go to the length of saying, so far as I am aware, that thought itself is a veil which prevents us from seeing reality. It is true that certain biographical details about Wittgenstein's life may point towards the latter, particularly when these are combined with his comments about the unspeakability of the mystical in the *Tractatus* period. It is interesting to note that Wittgenstein made the following comment to Friedrich Waismann in the Vienna Circle;

> I can well imagine a religion in which there are no doctrines, so that nothing is spoken. Clearly, then, the essence of religion can have nothing to do with what is said – or rather: if anything is said, then that itself is an element in religious behaviour, and not a *theory*.[85]

John Canfield has urged us to consider Zen Buddhism as just such a religion.[86] The same philosopher has also suggested we could see Wittgenstein's philosophy in an entirely new way by seeing, in terms of his analysis, language as an expression of the Tao. Wittgenstein's interpretation of language as 'patterned forms of just doing something'[87] grounded in the bedrock 'practice' is so close to speaking of language as an expression of the Tao as to make the equation 'seemingly inevitable' for Canfield. Whatever the experts make of these apparent affinities between Wittgenstein's approach and the mindless activity treasured by Buddhists, there clearly are both connections and disconnections.

AVOIDING THOUGHT, ALL APPEARS[88]

As we have seen, for Krishnamurti, true freedom is not having to decide – to be choicelessly aware – free from the shackles of thought and the known. Wittgenstein tries to free us from a conception of how we understand language, pointing out how there is a certain choicelessness about all our language/activity in our blind observance of the rule. We may see Wittgenstein's point but this by itself does not establish the more radical argument Krishnamurti is putting forward. Nevertheless, as I have suggested, it does support Krishnamurti's case to the degree that it sees the superfluity of thought in our understanding of language. The question is, however, whether the pure, thoughtless seeing, advocated by Krishnamurti, is a possible option in – following Wittgenstein – the thoughtless games we do actually play. The aphorism which heads this final section may be taken in two ways. From Krishnamurti's viewpoint, when we avoid thought all appears simply as it is in its pure, undescribed state. From Wittgenstein's position, when we avoid thought all appears more clearly through the practices we have chosen to adopt.

In the light of Wittgenstein's analysis it seems impossible to take up the critical approach to language as such which is implied in Krishnamurti's writings. Language can only be criticised from the standpoint of another language tradition. It cannot be criticised in the light of 'pure' thinking or observation. To have a language is *already* to be involved in an *agreement* about what is there to be seen. If this were the final word, the position argued for by Krishnamurti would be impossible. I shall leave the issue at that point for the moment and return to it later. I shall be content here to state the basic issue which divides the kind of views expressed by Krishnamurti and Wittgenstein. Although Krishnamurti is not writing consciously from a Hindu perspective, his thinking clearly expresses a view of language which is characteristically Indian. As Heinrich Zimmer observes;

> Indian philosophy is basically skeptical of words,

skeptical of their adequacy to render the main topic of philosophical thought, and therefore very cautious about trying to bring into a purely intellectual formula the answer to the riddle of the universe and man's existence. 'What is all this around me, this world in which I find myself? What is this process carrying me on, together with the earth? Whence has it all proceeded? Whither is it tending? And what is to be my role, my duty, my goal, amidst this bewildering breath-taking drama in which I found myself involved? That is the basic problem in the mind of men when they start philosophizing and before they reduce their aspirations to questions of methodology and the criticism of their own mental and sensual faculties.'[89]

Wittgenstein was critical of the philosopher's misuse of language and acknowledged that particular uses of language may be inadequate in some contexts. But he is not sceptical, in his later writings at least, of the adequacy of language as such. As I suggested at the end of the previous section, Wittgenstein's references to the ineffable and the mystical in his earlier period may point to a different possibility. However, I can only refer the reader here to an earlier discussion of mine which explores this particular problem in more detail.[90]

Despite the qualifications of the last paragraph we are bound to say that many who read Wittgenstein feel that they are listening to a Zen master. Writing to his friend Paul Engelmann during World War I Wittgenstein talks of how the ineffable may be contained in what is uttered. He concludes the letter:

> About your changeable mood: it is like this: We are asleep.... *Our* life is like a dream. But in our better hours we wake up just enough to realize that we are dreaming. Most of the time, though,

we are fast asleep. I cannot awaken myself! I am trying hard, my dream body moves, but my real one *does not stir*. This, alas, is how it is.[91]

Jacob Needleman shows how Wittgenstein's later writings may be understood as an exposure of the nature of this *sleep* in which we are caught.[92] Krishnamurti would say, I think, that Wittgenstein has vividly expressed the true nightmare of the dreamer trying to wake himself up but has underestimated how deep is the sleep.

3 Atheism in the name of God

I WROTE IN THE introduction that one of the aims of this study is to show the relevance of Alan Watts' thought to contemporary issues in religion. I shall never forget reading as a student these words from his autobiography, *In My Own Way*; 'Somehow I have come to a place where I see through ideas, beliefs, and symbols.'[93] This was one of the most refreshing passages I had read in years. A theologian, after all, deals in ideas, beliefs and symbols. They are the stuff of his trade. Yet here was someone who said quite casually that he had seen through them. I was so used to reading books by theologians expressing their tortured belief in belief that Alan Watts' approach seemed like water in the desert. Since pursuing his thought over the past few years it has become incomprehensible to me that the position he represents should be so little known in Great Britain, his native country. His writings are obviously more widely known in the United States but it would be a great pity if he were consigned to the history books already as a seminal figure in the consciousness boom of the sixties, an influential force in the Human Potentials movement and a reluctant guru to the flower people. This would be enough for anyone's lifetime but there is much in his life and thought which far transcends the fads of San Francisco.

Watts was very much influenced by Krishnamurti as books like *The Wisdom of Insecurity* show very clearly. The last chapter has hopefully prepared the ground for this part of the study and introduced a connection with Ludwig Wittgenstein

I want to pursue later in relation to Watts. Krishnamurti, however, showed no interest in confronting or exploring any of the religions in detail. There are many references to the absurdity of religious traditions and dogmas but he appears to have no taste for discussing how the deeper aspects of the traditions appear in the light of his own philosophy. By contrast, Alan Watts devoted much of his time to exploring the religions in relation to his own views. The hardline Krishnamurti would waste no time on such matters.

Alan Watts was once asked the question, 'What are you? A Christian? A Buddhist?' He replied, 'I'm here, can't you see what I am?' Watts died in 1973 and it would be against the whole spirit of his teachings to attempt to classify him now, after his death, in terms of any standard philosophical or religious position. He put his lifetime's preoccupation in what, for many, would be old-fashioned terms; 'the mystery of being is my supreme fascination'[94]. In one address he asked his audience to imagine that they were granted an interview with God during which they were allowed to ask one question. Watts' response to his own question was, 'I simply cannot formulate the question that contains my wonder.'[95] Nevertheless, he tried many ways to share his fascination with thinking people through lectures, books, essays and private classes. He wanted them 'to be more aware of the actual vibrations of life as they would listen to music.'[96] This is the major reason for his move away from Christianity towards Mahayana Buddhism, Taoist and Vedanta philosophy. Christianity had beauty but it lacked depth; 'I wanted to plumb and understand *being* itself, the very heart and ground of the universe, not to control it, but simply to wonder at it, for I was . . . amazed at my own existence.'[97]

Watts once compared his own activity of philosophizing to singing in the bathtub or splashing in the sea. It was philosophy in the spirit of the artist, celebrating the eternal and purposeless background of human life. On several occasions he admitted to being bored with the brand of modern philosophy which is simply about philosophy. Watts' approach was exactly suited to give intellectual expression to the hippie and consciousness movements of the sixties. For a time he became one of the most influential figures of the counter-culture, although he scoffed at the idea of being anybody's guru. When the musical *Hair* opened in San Francisco he was invited to lead the cast in mantra-chanting. Watts also appeared under a pseudonym in Kerouac's novel *The Dharma Bums*. In later years Watts lamented the way in which the beat generation had become aggressively dowdy and had caricatured his philosophy. He was always counter-cultural in terms of the standard religions and philosophical canons. He was an intellectual critic of the intellectual life. He did not despise the intellectual approach but only the meticulous drudgery, anal retention and condescension which often accompanies it. In what follows I shall not be concerned with the question of how far Watts' own teaching is faithful to any particular religious or philosophical tradition or with the degree to which it developed over his lifetime. There is an extensive list of Watts' writings in the bibliography at the end of this book.

LANGUAGE AS SEDUCTIVE GESTURE

A convenient way in to a discussion of Watts' thought is to pick up once more Aldous Huxley's distinction between humanity as the victim and as the beneficiary of its language systems. Throughout his writings Watts is acutely aware of the dual role of language. He often put the matter in the following way. Imagine the universe to be a gigantic rorschach blot, the real nature of which is unspeakable. On to this blot 'we are projecting the fantasies of personality, purpose, history, religion, law, science, evolution, and even the basic instinct to survive. And this projection is, in turn, part of the happening.'[98] Our words and language systems are, therefore, perfectly natural expressions or vibrations in the endlessly variegated vibrations of the cosmic rorschach blot; 'Words are just like the patterns of ferns or...the marks on sea shells.'[99] Language systems and the explanations of the world implicit in them are 'just another form of complexity, a new manifestation of life on top of life, a gesture gesturing.'[100] Words have the vital function of helping us to keep in mind the rules of the particular games we choose to play. Language embodies the shared agreements and constitutes the communication without which there would be no game. In this sense we are indeed the beneficiary. However, as Watts repeatedly points out, we easily become entranced or spellbound by our own words. He once wrote a book of nonsense as a playful attempt to overcome our slavery to words.[101] Many of his works are more formal efforts to accomplish the same thing. As he comments in his study of psychotherapy in eastern and western cultures;

> Language *seems* to be a system of fixed terms standing over against the physical events to which they refer.... Speaking and thinking are events in and of the physical world, but they are carried on *as if* they were outside it, as if they were an independent and fixed measure with which life could be compared.[102]

All thinking and speaking classifies the world and creates the illusion that the description *is* the real. The division of the world into things, events, knower and known, and so on is purely conventional. Language, therefore, is essentially divisive. For this reason Watts frequently includes language and thinking in his understanding of *maya* or unreality. It is not that the world itself is unreal but that language and thought systems are conventional. All language is geared to the realm of relativity and hence cannot describe what the world is in its absolute, non-verbal state. The very act of *saying* involves the assumption that existence is a collection of parts. Because the grammar and structure of language fragments the world into things and events, it cannot properly express what is implicit in it – the unity of differences, for example. It is paradoxical that we should have to describe the problem with the very language structure which gets us into it.

Religion is usually thought to be concerned with the truth about what is ultimately real, beyond all merely human ways of speaking about it. Religion has a natural interest in the universe in its absolute, non-verbal state. Does religion have a non-verbal access to the ultimately real which avoids the snares of language? The first part of an answer to this question must be a negative one. To adopt an illustration Watts occasionally uses, a mirror is the indispensable ground of the images it reflects, but it cannot itself be described in terms of the shapes and colours of those images. More positively, we can, according to Watts, *sense* the absolute nature of the world in mystical states of consciousness, an 'inverse or obverse of the view of the world given in our divisive language forms.'[103] In his early writings Watts included all such experiences under the term 'metaphysic' (i.e. in the singular), experiences in which we apprehend reality 'directly and immediately, as distinct from what we know by reflection, inference and abstraction.'[104] In the very strictest sense, therefore, 'metaphysic' does not have a language. As we saw when discussing Krishnamurti, it is just such claims as these which would cause all the modern sceptical prickles to rise. Watts, like Krishnamurti, defends the possibility of human-beings having a direct, untranslated sense of the world. For both philosophers, words are incantations which spellbind us into thinking that the description of the world is somehow the world itself. Words are real, but the reality to which they refer is not itself an idea. Life imitates the language and we are seduced into thinking that the world, like words, is *about* something else.

MAYA — REALITY AS SOCIALLY APPROVED

If the universe is a rorschach blot the projections on to it are *maya*. All thought and language about it is projection. There is no neutral, pure language which describes it simply as it is. We may indeed ask 'What is reality?' but every answer is classification. There is no point in protesting by saying that everyone knows that the world *is* 'physical,' 'material,' and so on. These descriptions are themselves *philosophical ideas*. Physical and material are words we use to talk *about* the world. The world as it is in itself is unspeakable. The words we use about the world embody our conventional ways of thinking. Conventions are 'conveniences' and we readily acknowledge this to be the case in systems of measurement, legal and social customs, and so on. Yet every way we speak about the world is conventional. Watts would say, with Max Müller, that things are 'thinks.' There are no things in the world. Things are terms, not entities. All things, facts and events are simplified, convenient units of perception and attention. They represent how much of the real world we are able to grasp with the separate ideas of conscious attention. The pigeon holes are in the mind and not in reality. The world is fragmented only by thought. Conscious attention seduces us into forgetting this. We therefore imagine that the separate bits need to be connected in some way – hence the idea that one event causes another. But, of course, there are no separate events. There is just one total happening. To speak of separate events is to attend to different aspects of one continuous happening. This is why Watts suggests at times that it would be better to call the world spiritual rather than material. To be unspiritual is to impose 'thingness' and separateness on the world.

Watts' general outlook could certainly be classified as mystical if a classification is needed. It should not be supposed, however, that what he says about language dissolves everything into an infinite mushy sea of jelly. This could not be further from the truth. Yet it is often in the mind of people when they hear the word mystical. A simple example makes the point. In a recent televised interview, the British politician Tony Benn was asked about his attitude towards religion. He replied that he was very involved in the theological enterprise in so far as it is concerned with human behaviour and changing social structures. He added that he was not interested at all in what he called the mystical side of religion. This is quite a common observation. The implication is that mystical experience is superfluous to the real business of religion, even a sign of self-indulgence, an escape from the real world.

A sustained reading of Watts' writings reveals just how superficial such a view of mysticism can be. The mistaken assumption is that mystical experience represents a retreat into a purely 'subjective' state of consciousness. On the contrary, the mystical state of mind is one in which we are far more acutely aware of the world as it actually *is* as distinct from what we *think* and *say* about it. What we usually call the real or everyday world is, in fact, more 'subjective' than the mystical state; the everyday world is the abstract and conceptual one. It cloaks an unexamined philosophical sub-conscious in which we compulsively symbolize to ourselves, under socially approved orders, what we think is going on. The following observation by Watts indicates the relevance and the general thrust of most of his writings; 'Western man needs to be turned outside-in, to live in the real world which he thinks is abstract, instead of the abstract world which he takes for reality.'[105] The mystical state is a liberation from the social and conventional realities, from *maya*. As Aldous Huxley comments, Jews and gipsies were murdered by the Nazis because they were categorized as 'Jews' and 'gipsies.' The mystical state would have seen them as they were, not as illustrations of an idea.[106]

THE PSYCHIC CHAUFFEUR AND THE REAL NATURE
OF THE SELF

Most of Alan Watts' writings are concerned in varying ways with one central, fundamental experience; that of trans-formed identity. It is polar awareness, seeing that what you do and what happens to you are aspects of the same process.

By contrast, ordinary waking consciousness separates these sharply into the voluntary and the involuntary. In his autobiography Watts goes so far as to say that his whole work in religion and philosophy has been to convey this feeling of transformed identity to others; 'that whatever it is, I am that, and whatever I am is also what stars and galaxies, space and energy are.'[107] Watts recalls that this feeling has been obvious to him as long as he could remember. Yet this experience is not a common one. In his book, *Does It Matter?*, he includes this succinct summary;

> Almost all civilized peoples have been brought up to think of themselves...as skin-encapsulated egos, or as psychic chauffeurs in mechanical vehicles of flesh and bone. We have learned to identify ourselves exclusively with that part of the brain which functions as a sort of radar or scanning apparatus and which is the apparent center of conscious attention and voluntary action.[108]

It is this assumed identity, based on the experience of conscious attention which Watts devoted his energies to transforming. The serial or narrowed consciousness is basic to modern western peoples' self-understanding yet it is 'as alien to the natural man as was the supernatural soul.'[109] It is obvious that Watts was influenced in his view of consciousness by the Taoist philosophy with its emphasis on the seamless unity of nature which does not involve the loss of personal identity. Watts was influenced too by the Hindu and Buddhist spiritual disciplines as ways of realizing the self as a process far vaster than what is usually and superficially experienced to be I. He is asking us to locate the centre of ourselves at a deeper and more universal level than we are accustomed to do. In many of his writings he relentlessly asks his reader to become aware of the conventional distinction between what we usually call 'self' and 'other.' Where is the dividing line? 'Do you draw the line at just that much of you which you are aware of, just that much which your consciousness can catch hold of?... The question is, how much of yourself can you catch hold of, and who is doing the catching?'[110]

Like Krishnamurti, Watts argues that we usually identify ourselves with an idea we have of ourselves – the ego. We are actually in a completely fluid situation and yet we feel that it somehow 'clots' with us. We identify ourselves with what we take to be a fixed form, a construction of memories we call 'I.' What we normally feel to be 'self' is a mere phantom which disappears when we stop symbolizing to ourselves. It is an abstraction based on memory. In saying all of this, however, we should understand that Watts is not making a moralistic accusation against egotism. He is not writing in the spirit of the preacher condemning people in general for a moral fault. To identify yourself with an abstraction from memory is to fall for a conceptual illusion, rather than to commit sin. Furthermore, to want to put the matter right in the same ego mode of consciousness is to compound the illusion. The ego can only be taught to be egoistic. Watts sometimes compares the normal ego state to a quaking mess. The desire to be ego-less is simply an appetite within the quaking mess. While it is an illusory state it is, nevertheless, not a harmless illusion. To feel inwardly isolated from the natural world is to be potentially hostile and aggressive towards it. It is easy to see the harmful effects of twentieth century technology guided as it is by egocentric consciousness.

What, we may ask, can be done, granted that an illusion cannot get rid of illusion? Watts' answer to this question has to be assessed in the light of the possibility of an enlightened state of consciousness which is at the heart of his teachings and which is the subject of the next section. Most of his output can be seen as an attempt to answer the question. His writings, in total, are a form of intellectual yoga, overcoming thought by thought itself. As a philosopher he is attempting to dispel the illusions of language by using the very language that bewitches us.

THAT THAN WHICH THERE IS NO WHICHER

As I suggested earlier, Watts' whole approach depends on the possibility of a pure, untranslated, direct experience of the world and the transformed sense of identity which accompanies it. It is the possibility of what he called 'metaphysic' – the direct, immediate apprehension of reality before any notion of fact, symbol, event, and so on enters in. This experience is 'prefactual' in contrast to what we know by abstraction, inference and reflection. It is important to grasp Watts' meaning here. He is not speaking about uninterpreted sense-data. He is making a much more fundamental point. To assume that sense-data are the foundations of experience is a philosophical opinion, *already* based on memory and reflection. Watts dropped the term metaphysic in later years but his original choice of the term brings out the essential point. It is knowledge of what is 'beyond nature'; that is, of what 'we experience before we ascertain the *nature* of our experiences by reflection – by remembering, naming, and classifying.'[111] As Watts readily acknowledged, 'metaphysic' so defined is without a language; it is ineffable in the strictest sense. We cannot know *about* this experience in the way we know about things which form part of our memory and systems of reflective thought. In the conventional, ordinary sense, all knowledge is memory, knowledge of that which was.

One of the reasons why we resist the possibility of a direct apprehension of the world is that we fail to see the indirect nature of our normal state of consciousness. The latter feels as though it were as direct an apprehension as we could get. After all, are we not naturally self-conscious? It is just this that Watts challenges. To say that we know that we know is just another way of saying that we arrive late for the feast, to use the image I applied to Krishnamurti's teachings. While I am thinking thought x, I am not aware *that* I am aware of thought x. 'I am aware that I am thinking thought x' is no longer thought x, but thought y. Thought y is not thought x;

it is my memory of *having had* thought *x*. I am, therefore, never aware of a self or ego which *has* a present experience. Every attempt to be aware of being aware is a vicious circle, an infinite regress of illusions. However much I speak of the 'present moment,' it is a specious present – a memory of the immediate past. What we take as direct experience is usually a *record* of it. Our normal state of awareness is a form of reflective consciousness. It is the bookkeeping side of the business but not the business itself. The real business, the present world with which we are essentially and totally at one, cannot be remembered and is never an object of knowledge.

Let me elaborate a little. The universe evokes us at birth as conscious beings. Consciousness as we normally experience it does not illuminate its own origin. We feel that there is something of a 'gap' separating us from the universe. By accepting a system of symbols about the world and of our own identity we come to terms with the universe with greater or lesser degrees of success. There is a whole vocabulary – all too familiar – which goes with the various strategies for negotiating the 'gap.' We are urged to 'face up' to reality, recognize 'hard facts,' 'conquer' space, and so on. The point is, however, that the celebrated gap is merely a conventional distinction. Our languages, thoughts and ideas need not be treated as connecting devices. So understood, however successfully they seem to connect us with the universe, they will be experienced as a block. When we see through the conventional division between us and the world, words, thoughts and ideas appear as natural as flowers or as hairs growing from the head. Conscious attention itself can be seen in the same natural way. As Watts observes; 'We don't think before we think, and we don't know how we think: we just do it.'[112] To put the process of thinking in this context frees it from the aura of strain. The universe never will be comprehended by conscious thought. Universal knowledge would have to include the thinking about the thinking, and who is going to think about that? As Watts points out, there is a givenness about consciousness and knowing which simply has to be accepted if we are to avoid the futile pursuits of trying to know how we know; 'How can we know what we know without knowing knowing?'[113]

Watts calls this feeling that we are one with everything that is *The Supreme Identity* which is, incidentally, the title of one of his more technical works. The experience of the unremembered moment, the eternal now, cosmic consciousness – or whatever term we use – does not, as I have said before, have a language. It is to be in the non-verbal dimension of consciousness. Yet there are analogies of the experience which approximate to the absolute character of this dimension. On Watts' view, it is the religions of the world which provide us with the analogies. The language of such analogies must not be mistakenly taken as having a factual or hypothetical status. Where the analogies are treated in this way they belong to 'metaphysics' (i.e. in the plural); 'as if they were facts on a higher level of objective existence than sensually perceptible things.'[114] By contrast, their deep and true status is 'metaphysic' which Watts regards as the indefinable basis of knowledge;

> Metaphysical knowledge or 'realization' is an intense clarity of attention to that indefinable and immediate 'point' of knowledge which is always 'now,' and from which all other knowledge is elaborated by reflective thought. A consciousness of 'life' in which the mind is not trying to grasp or define what it knows.[115]

It is obvious that some religious analogies are more naturally expressive of this state of realization than others. Watts continuously draws on the eastern faiths and philosophies for this reason. They are more amenable than the western religions in showing realization as a present fact rather than as a future attainment. Watts' elaboration of the meaning of the Hindu *Tat Tvam Asi* (that are thou) lies at the centre of his approach in showing his readers that they may feel themselves as one particular focal point where the whole universe is expressing itself; the only real self is the whole. He is also fond of using the phrase *sat-chit-ananda* which I mentioned in the last chapter when discussing Krishnamurti. Watts translates this phrase as 'the which than which there is no whicher' to stress that – if only we could see it – our ordinary state of life now is the ultimate state of bliss. We are standing right now in the middle of the Beatific Vision. Writing as a religious philosopher, Watts' aim was to help his readers to *feel* and not merely to understand this deep sense of transformed identity. *The Book on the Taboo Against Knowing Who You Are* was written for this purpose and supplements his more technical *The Supreme Identity*. The universe is a game. All beings are the masks and plays of the central Self.

BELIEF, FAITH AND THE REALITY OF GOD

This exposition of Watts' thought has been very cursory, as readers of his considerable output will readily see. It may, however, have provided a rough and ready framework for those unfamiliar with his writings and who intend to read him themselves. Watts' presentation of his material, like Krishnamurti's, is well outside the standard grooves and this may have left some readers of the present book a little puzzled. Such people may rightly wish to ask the kind of straightforward questions raised when Krishnamurti was discussed: Does Watts believe in God? What are we to make of faith and belief? Is religion just a form of projection? I shall now turn to questions like these.

Watts was not a purist on religion as Krishnamurti seems to be and gives much fuller answers to the type of question I have just introduced. Let us recall to begin with Watts' assertion that the direct, immediate apprehension of reality is the supreme, absolute experience for a human being. Religious knowledge is an analogy of this experience; it is 'mediate, objective and analogical.'[116] Religious symbols and doctrines may even be thought of as projections without this being understood in the reductionist Feuerbachian or Freudian sense. Our deep inner centre – the supreme self in Watts' terms – is 'making itself incarnate, or projecting itself, into the exterior world of variety and multiplicity.'[117] This is perfectly natural on Watts' view. Everything can be seen as a gesture of the divine, so why not thoughts and language systems? They are gestures gesturing. Confusion arises, however, when those symbols and doctrines are thought to point to an *external* reality. They are inevitably interpreted in this way in a culture dominated by the ego-centre type of consciousness. God, it is thought, must be an object of knowledge, however elusive this may be to define. This raises all the problems of belief so familiar to us in the debates about religion throughout the past century. Belief, according to Watts, plays a very problematic role in the context of the central experience we are discussing here.

Alexis Preyre said, 'I thought that what separated me from God was doubt. But perhaps it was belief.' Watts would approve of this observation. Belief and faith are commonly treated as synonyms. Watts treats them as opposites. Belief is a barrier to true faith and realization. The latter 'needs no belief, for we can only believe in what we have already known, preconceived and imagined.'[118] To talk of belief in the same breath as God is to deny from the start the very reality God is supposed to have. It implies the desire to pin God down or possess him conceptually. As we have seen, for Watts all thinking is classification. To think about something is to put it into a class of things and give it a boundary. We observe what we call the world and our mind breaks it up into events, things, facts and so on. We do not see events, things and facts in the first place. These are a product of the splintering process of the mind. Not to see that this is what happens is to suppose, inevitably, that if God is to be real then he too must be some sort of fact. Our mind conceives differences – this fact, that thing, those events – and we suppose that God must be one of those differences – a really hard fact and the most important of the differences. As Watts comments; 'the theologians really want to say that God is a fact, a thing – albeit the first fact and the first thing, the Being before all beings.'[119] Just as the remembered moment misses the absolute nature of our true selves, so concepts of God are groping in an area where he can never be found. Concepts of God, like ideas of ourselves are just a little late and miss the feast. The theologians have rationalized God and 'degraded him to the level of a dead, fixed thing – dead because all things are past, inhabiting only the world of memory.'[120] The person who once said that theology was a rarefied form of atheism was no fool.

Watts was frequently accused of pantheism because of the contents of theological books such as *Behold the Spirit, Myth and Ritual in Christianity* and the more recent *Beyond Theology*. This charge, however, is an expression of the theological state of mind which Watts wishes to expose as inadequate. It would be absurd, on Watts' view, to identify God with those 'things' which only exist in a verbal and conventional sense. It is, in fact, the more traditional theologians who are 'unconscious pantheists' in trying to identify God with a concept, some special state of mind, and so on.[121] God becomes the ego of the universe. All ideas and concepts of God are, in one sense, a denial of the reality of God. Because they are more abstract than images and pictures they are more dangerous. They are much more likely to be taken for the real thing, whether it be Tillich's 'ground of being' or Northrop's 'undifferentiated aesthetic continuum.' Faith, as Watts understands it, does not require concepts of any kind to hold on to. It is complete letting go. For this reason faith 'is not in or upon anything at all.'[122] It has no tangible content in terms of a system of beliefs. It is direct realization and this experience does not need a concept of itself, just as an individual does not need an idea of himself or the sun to shine on itself. Alan Watts, speaking in his role as a theologian, wanted to wipe off the pictures and concepts of God from the windows of our minds. They get in the way of the reality we fondly assume they define. Many may feel that this is an odd preoccupation for a theologian. I shall conclude this chapter by showing that this is far from being a perverse activity and, incidently, summarize Watts' approach in relation to the general theological enterprise.

THE THEOLOGIANS — PEOPLE OF DISTINCTIONS

There have been two main trends in the use of religious language by theologians. One way is the use of positive language to say what God is *like* and is usually called cataphatic theology. The second way is the use of negative language to speak in terms of what God is *not* like. This *via negativa* is called apophatic theology or the way of remotion. If we wish to locate Watts in the long tradition of theology it would be in the second category and in the spirit of that found particularly in *Theologia Mystica* of Saint Dionysius.[123] As I commented earlier, Watts' religious and philosophical writings take the form of an intellectual yoga, a purification of the senses from their slavery to concepts. The resulting state of consciousness is, in Indian terms, *samadhi*, the purest form of which is *nirvikalpa samadhi*, that is, *nir-*(non-) *vikalpa* (conceptual). If religious words and symbols are to have deep roots to them, and not merely be on the level of conventional distinctions, they must ultimately be expressive of this state of consciousness. I shall take up this issue in a later chapter when I discuss Watts' thought in relation to that of Ludwig Wittgenstein. It is sufficient to make the point here that Watts thinks that God has been trivialized by theologians in their tendency to project him into the world of objects and conventional distinctions. It is hardly surprising that Watts is very critical of theologians at many points. His criticism was particularly severe of theology in general in his *Myth and Ritual in Christianity*; 'it is the product of a mentality still very much under the spell of illusion.'[124] For Watts, theologians even of

the most contemporary kind are too easily spellbound by the
conventions and distinctions which the central experience of
realization is meant to transcend. This is the vital and much
neglected contribution Watts has made to modern theology.
He sets himself against both the traditionalist and contemporary camps in theology. He is critical of the orthodox
theologians who still put forward a God in the form of a
cosmic eastern potentate and also of those who speak of ultimate reality in less crude and vaguer terms.

In his introduction to *The Perennial Philosophy* Aldous
Huxley makes a pertinent remark about the blindness of what
he called empirical theologians which is highly relevant to the
point I am making here. Modern astronomers, he observes,
would never dream of relying on the unaided eye of someone
studying the constellation of Orion, something appearing as
as faint smudge without a telescope. He continues; 'Natural
science is empirical; but it does not confine itself to the
experience of human beings in their merely human and
unmodified condition. Why empirical theologians should feel
themselves obliged to submit to this handicap, goodness only
knows.'[125] It is exactly this handicap which Watts has refused
to accept and which makes his work stand against the grain
and which, incidentally, makes it so relevant in the best sense.
If we do need a new understanding of God, we need at the
same time a new understanding of what it means to be
ourselves at a far deeper level than that assumed in the
academic debates in the fields of theology and philosophy.
Watts summarized his own contribution in the following
way;

> I have advocated something called atheism in the
> name of God. That is to say, an experience, a
> contact, a relationship to God with the ground of
> your being, that does not have to be embodied or
> expressed in any specific image.[126]

We have to be careful to understand Watts here. As the last
few paragraphs should have made clear, he does not fit into

any of the death of God or secular theology schools, both brands of which he found particularly unimaginative and wishy washy. Rather, he was trying to elaborate upon, through the divisive medium of language itself, an *experience* of God rather than refine a *concept* of God which would be acceptable to the modern mind. There is nothing of the latter intellectual strain in Watts. Theologians have been spell-bound into confusing the meaning of religion with its form; 'when asked to explain the meaning they give only a more detailed exposition of the form.' The form of Christianity in its intellectual aspect is doctrine. Watts is concerned with the 'meaning of God himself, the ultimate Reality, not as an idea conceived but as a reality experienced.'[127]

One of the aims of this chapter has been to discuss Watts' thought in a way which pointed towards the possibility of a new kind of theological critique. Watts himself felt that he was too close to the very varied context of his own work to assess its distinctive contribution.[128] At times, however, he does admit that there are the seeds of a new, exciting depar-ture in theology in his own writings. He used the term 'metatheology' for this new approach.[129] Metatheology would not be a polemic or a restatement in contemporary terms. It would rather treat theology as a *form of life*. Not as something *about* life, but as a natural expression of life, as natural as a species of flower or bird. This would be com-bined with what Alan Watts called the Chinese box approach, illuminating 'one theological system...by looking at it and seeing what happens to it in the context of another.'[130] The Chinese box, for Watts, was the whole spectrum of the world's religions and philosophies, which makes his approach very opportune in the light of the new interest in dialogue between religions. Alan Watts had the ability to get deep down into ways of thinking quite strange to the western mind. To those unfamiliar with them, the eastern religions can appear as great edifices of bewildering beliefs and unpro-nounceable terminologies. They are, indeed, fantastic architectures of thought which, some would say, are not for westerners to inhabit.[131] Watts is much more optimistic than this, without, however, advocating a chop suey religion concocted by a mixture of faiths. The truth is that, for many, Christianity takes on a dimension of new depth when seen in the light of another religion. We know what a Hellenized Christianity looks like. It has been with us for two millenia. What would an Orientalized Christianity be like? Alan Watts' writings offer many pointers to how Christianity would appear if if were more profoundly influenced by Vedanta, Buddhism and Taoism.

Let me summarize the negative and positive aspects of Watts' contribution to the theological debate. Theology, as normally conducted, has come to a dead end. Theologians are prospecting an exhausted mine. Theological thinking has followed the method of enquiry found in western academic philosophy with its stress on the verbalization of experience. It has entered the vicious circle of attempting to *think thought*, constructing words about words about words.[132] The underlying assumption of many books on philosophical theology is that if only we could get the ideas right, reality and God would be truly illuminated. Such writings do contain some psychological insights but rarely any real surprises. The doctrines are always *about* something else; they are fingers pointing to other realities. Some suck them for comfort while others follow the direction of the finger into the bright blue yonder in the hope that it points to a some sort of a something somewhere. There is, however, another way of understanding Christian doctrines. If we see the self less exclusively as an isolated individual consciousness, and more in terms of the matrix from which it emerges, the doctrines acquire a subterranean richness of meaning denied to them in an exclusively western and Christian context. We gain an entirely different perspective for their meaning. The doctrines and theologies become in themselves expressions of a realized state. Their status is changed by the wider setting. They embody possibilities for understanding consciousness and the sensation of the self outside the conventions which normally mark out the perimeters of western theology. Before pursuing Watts' thought further I shall examine a development in religious thinking which comes close to seeing theological uses of language as themselves expressions of religious truth.

4   *Letting it be*

AT THE END OF THE last chapter I drew attention to the possibility of a new kind of theological critique in the style of Alan Watts' approach. This would be to treat theology as a *form of life*, a form of existence in itself rather than a commentary on existence. 'Thoughts grow in brains as grass grows in fields'[133] and some of these thoughts are theological. Let theology be itself. It is difficult to be yourself in a courtroom, yet this is often the assumed context for academic discussions in theology and the philosophy of religion. The tone is apologetic, polemical and testy. The theologians and religious philosophers have been in dialogue with western unbelief for so long that the habit is difficult to break. However, as I suggested in the introduction, there are welcome signs of relief from this brand of claustrophobia in the work of Ludwig Wittgenstein and his followers. It is very significant that much of the most lively and interesting religious thinking in the past few decades has come from this group which has not seen its task as that of justifying religion before a higher sceptical authority.[134] Alan Watts' work was produced in a quite different context from that which we associate with the Wittgensteinian approach. Much of Watts' material predated this recent trend in any case. Nevertheless, it seems to me that the philosophical approach of Wittgenstein and the religious thinking of Watts throw a great deal of light on each other. For this reason I shall devote most of this chapter to an outline of Wittgenstein's significance for the present discussion.

I shall begin by picking up the quotation from Wittgenstein

in the introduction. Wittgenstein wondered whether words discussed by philosophers are 'ever actually used in this way in the language-game which is its original home?'[135] He commented that his own practice is to bring them back from their metaphysical to their everyday use. Philosophers, according to Wittgenstein, unconsciously introduce notions into the material they discuss which do not belong there. Instead of analyzing language in the context from which it derives its meaning – its original home – philosophers impose their own distorting 'metaphysical' usage. As we saw earlier, his own advice is 'don't think, but look!' If we ask where we are to look to find the clue to the true home or essence of language usage, Wittgenstein tells us to examine the 'grammar.' '*Essence* is expressed by grammar'[136] and again, 'Grammar tells what kind of object anything is.'[137] Yet we might still wonder how we are to avoid the distorted or metaphysical interpretation of the grammar.

The grammar of any particular use of language is the framework within which that usage derives its sense and non-sense. The best way to understand grammar, says Wittgenstein, is to pay close attention to the role the language actually has in the lives of the people who use it. The task of philosophers is simply to analyze what they find. They cannot go beyond this without advocating in a way which puts them out of role. As Wittgenstein observes:

> Philosophy may in no way interfere with the actual use of language; it can in the end only describe it. For it cannot give it any foundation either. It leaves everything as it is.[138]

Wittgenstein's own method for paying close attention simply to what is said and there to be seen has involved the notions of language games and forms of life. They are very familiar terms in philosophical discussions these days. A great deal of argument still continues over their technical meaning and the range of their application. There is no space, however, to enter those detailed debates here. It is sufficient for the present purposes simply to say that a language game is a use of language embodied in practices in a way which gives it a peculiar sense. Great care is necessary to locate the different senses involved in the various language games; 'We remain unconscious of the prodigious diversity of all the everyday language-games because the clothing of our language makes everything alike.'[139] Wittgenstein lists language games which include asking, thanking, cursing, greeting, reporting an event, and so on. These particular uses of language obviously run through many diverse practices. Imagine, for example, the different senses involved in the practice of thanking the milkman, lucky stars and God. It is the agreement and shared meanings in these particular activities which rule out the possibility of rootless language games; 'It is what human beings say that is true and false; and they agree in the *language* they use. That is not agreement in opinions but in form of life.'[140] The phrase 'form of life' is meant to bring out the collective agreements about the meaning involved in uses of language. Certain opinions may be mistaken, but the criteria for saying so is part of the given in the form of life; 'What has to be accepted, the given, is – so one could say – *forms of life.*'[141]

What happens when we use this approach to language in our analysis of religious belief? One of the chief aims would be to locate a genuinely religious utterance in view of the fact that the 'clothing of our language makes everything alike.' To do so we need to make use of another distinction Wittgenstein used, namely that of *surface* and *depth* grammar.[142] It is only by investigating the depth grammar, the deep assumptions in shared meanings, that we can tell whether a use of language is being used in a distinctively religious sense. In saying this we are already in the realm of controversy. Many would question the sense of speaking of a distinctively religious use of language. Whatever the case, Wittgenstein's followers are anxious to show how there may be uses of language which embody possibilities of religious meaning for people's lives, uses which are not other kinds of use in disguise.[143]

Closely linked with the search for language expressing genuine religion is the term 'picture.' People have, it is said, pictures which embody the possibilities for religious meaning. The term is not meant in a representational sense, although believers may, of course, have images of those meanings in their minds. Picture, rather, denotes the logical space or framework within which the distinctions of what it does and does not make sense to say may be drawn. As Wittgenstein comments; 'When I say he's using a picture I'm merely making a *grammatical* remark: [what I say] can only be verified by the consequences he does or does not draw.'[144] It is important to add too that these pictures are absolutes for the believer. They do not rest on something else more substantial than what is expressed through them. If the pictures die, for whatever reason, something irreplaceable dies with them.

Talk of pictures in relation to religious belief is closely connected with what Wittgenstein says in *On Certainty* about world pictures. Our world picture is that assumed framework within which we build a world with all its levels of truth and falsity and distinctions of sense and nonsense; 'it is the substratum of all my enquiry and asserting.'[145] Our world pictures are groundless in the sense that we assume them as the necessary background for any distinction we draw. If I attempt to point to the foundations of my world picture I must be assuming a still wider picture which I take for granted as groundless. The world picture I attempt to defend in this way has, in fact, crumbled. I cannot, in other words, say anything about my world picture which is more certain than that already implied in it.

If what I have said so far about Wittgenstein's approach has a bearing on our understanding of religion, and I believe it does, then the consequences are significant and far reaching. It raises the whole question of the autonomy of religious belief, and, by implication, all the issues of knowledge, truth and verification. One of the major thrusts in the writings of Wittgenstein's followers is that a failure to recognize the distinctions I have discussed so far in this chapter has led to philosophers importing notions, factual and referential ones for example, which are alien to the religious form of life. In short, philosophers have isolated religious uses of language from their original home and misunderstood them. Wittgenstein and his followers try to reverse this trend and analyze the language in its 'everyday use.' We should be careful not to misunderstand this phrase. They are not urging the philosopher to become folksy. 'Everyday' is not meant in the sense of routine, repetitious, obvious, banal. Indeed, the philosopher may discover that religious meanings, when seen in the context of their original home, do not have an everyday, familiar meaning at all.

What the Wittgensteinian view amounts to is this. We must give up what Wittgenstein himself called the craving for generality. This means realizing the futility of a search for a general and theoretical framework by use of which we can judge one world picture to be truer than another. We cannot set two or more world pictures alongside each other and determine their relative truth in the light of a perspective broader than both of them. Truth, in other words, is a context-dependent notion. The difference between truth and falsity, the real and the unreal, depends upon the world picture. As I noted at the outset of this chapter, Wittgenstein wonders whether terms like 'knowledge,' 'I,' etc. are used in the way philosophers often assume when they discuss religion. We may be said to know that the sun is at the centre of our solar system, but what does it mean to know God? Indeed, is the 'I' who knows the sun's position the same 'I' who knows God?

Some readers will suspect, of course, that the very act of drawing attention to different uses of language and the shared meanings makes the Wittgensteinian approach implausible, certainly as it is applied to religion. After all, it was the master himself who drew attention to the interdependence of language games. He pointed to 'a complicated network of similarities overlapping and criss-crossing; sometimes overall similarities, sometimes similarities of detail.'[146] Is there not, then, a means within the Wittgensteinian scheme of things of exposing the interdependence of world pictures, even those which appear radically dissimilar? What could this be? Why not language itself? Since everyone uses it, is it not reasonable to suppose that language has universal characteristics which take different forms in the admittedly distinctive uses? This really amounts to the following question; is it possible to obtain a normative definition of language games? If the answer is yes then it would be possible to draw up common criteria and judge whether a particular use of language was a misuse and a meaningless utterance.

In Wittgenstein's terms this is a request for the 'essence' of language. He called this the great question. He imagines someone reading the early paragraphs of the *Philosophical Investigations* and making the following protest;

> You take the easy way out! You talk about all sorts of language-games, but have nowhere said what the essence of a language-game, and hence of language, is.'[147]

Does Wittgenstein answer his own question? He does, and the answer is that it is a pointless, misleading request. It is certainly natural enough to feel that language is basically ordinary and that it is put to use for a great variety of purposes. I have mentioned the following statement in a different study but it is worth quoting again here to see just how beguiling is the desire for an essence of language. R.H. Bell comments; 'Language has a variety of uses, and people who speak a language frequently use that language for religious purposes.'[148] What could be simpler? Yet it is just such an observation which is at the root, I would say, of much reductionism in the discussion of religion. Bell and many others like him are really denying that religious language has an original home to be taken back to. In their view religion is borrowing a common coinage which hides the distinctively religious uses. This way of analyzing the issue blurs the grammatical distinctions Wittgenstein was anxious to preserve.

The point can be made by observing two distinctive uses of the same word in the context of actions judged to be good and bad in two different settings.[149] 'Ought' is the word in question. Consider the following dialogue. We are watching a friend play tennis and say:

'You ought to want to play better.'

He replies; 'I know I'm playing badly but I don't want to play any better.'

We say; 'Ah, then that's all right.'

Later the same day we observe the same friend commit a mean act and say;

'You ought to want to behave better.'

He replies; 'I know I behave badly, but then I don't want to behave any better.'

In these circumstances we could hardly say, 'Ah, then that's all right.' Since we criticized him for his behaviour we would be much more likely to say, 'Well you *ought* to want to behave better.' There is a clear distinction between the word ought as it is applied to bad tennis play and as it is applied to mean behaviour. The former usage embodies a *relative* and the latter an *absolute* judgement of value. In both cases, it is true, we were engaged in what Wittgenstein would call the language game of commending. Does it make sense, however, to say that our separate criticisms of the friend's actions were two instances of the *same* thing – commending? The word *ought* as it applied to a poor tennis performance carried a prudential, relative meaning. When the word was used to criticize the friend's behaviour it had an absolute moral sense. There are individuals, no doubt, who use *ought* prudentially even in a moral sense, but this does not affect the point being made here. Those, on the one hand, who use *ought* prudentially and those, on the other, who use it in an absolute sense are using the same *words* but they are speaking a different *language*. Their world pictures are different. They say different things. There is no broader perspective constructed by means of an alleged common language which could assimilate the two outlooks. They may still talk to each other, of course. Where their conversation is about the very bedrock of their moral convictions it takes, to use Wittgenstein's term, the form of 'reminders' which are themselves expressions of the intellectual distance involved. He gives a well known example of a conversation showing how close two people can be on ordinary matters and how distant on the subject of their fundamental world pictures;

> Suppose someone were a believer and said: 'I believe in a Last Judgement,' and I said: 'Well, I'm not so sure. Possibly.' You would say that there is an enormous gulf between us. If he said 'There is a German aeroplane overhead,' and I said 'Possibly. I'm not so sure,' you'd say we were fairly near.[150]

In their efforts to elucidate the truth or otherwise of the religious position, the Wittgensteinians have delved into the heart of the religious traditions themselves rather than attempt to satisfy what we could call external criteria. They have interpreted religious beliefs internally. The true home of religious statements is, after all, religion. This particular aspect of their output has been strongly criticized and much misunderstood. The major accusation is that they have severed the links religion has with the life of the world and the state of public knowledge; hence the label 'fideism.' It would, of course, be absurd to say that religion could be cut off from spheres, local or widely cultural ones and retain its meaning. As far as I am aware no Wittgensteinian has ever advocated this. Indeed, Wittgenstein himself observed that 'some language games become obsolete and get forgotten.' Changes in the life of man erode the possibility of holding on to certain beliefs. They die when the conditions which nourished them die;

> It is always a tragic thing when a language dies. But it doesn't follow that one can do anything to stop it doing so. It is a tragic thing when the love between a man and wife is dying; but there is nothing one can do. So it is with a dying language.[151]

This echoes a similar telling remark by C.S. Lewis; 'Men do not long continue to think what they have forgotten how to say.'[152]

In no sense then is Wittgenstein sanctioning a nature reserve for religious life and thought. The so-called 'internal' analysis is precisely to determine what the nature of the connections are with 'external' realities. It is doubtful in any case that a mature religious outlook would classify anything in the universe, let alone the native culture, as external to the religious experience. Nevertheless, many are bound to say that the Wittgensteinians have succumbed to the outlook of secular humanism despite their alleged concern to allow religion to be itself. The criticism is likely to run in this way. The Wittgensteinians are merely followers of intellectual fashion. They have abandoned the objective or realistic God out there because critical thinkers in general no longer talk of an objective world to be encountered by sensitive minds. It is not that there is a solid *reality* there to which our theories increasingly approximate with varying success. Rather, reality or what is thought to be real, changes as the theories change. To use the jargon, objectivism is theory – dependent. Our attention then is directed away from what is naively thought to be out there to the ways in which our theories project the realism appropriate to the theory. This general trend obviously runs through many branches of knowledge. In certain schools of psychology, for example, it is held that what we experience as 'out there' is identical to, or isomorphic with, our brain processes. The Wittgensteinians have brought religious statements home from their metaphysical to their everyday use but there is no one at home. They may well have released the philosopher's grip on religion. He is no longer the arbiter who decides whether religious language corresponds with metaphysical facts. Why has this happened? Because there are no metaphysical facts to which the religious statements *could* correspond.

The last paragraph is a crude summary of the kind of reaction Wittgenstein's modern followers evoke from their

opponents. Most of the criticism has been directed towards
Professor D.Z. Phillips of Swansea but in very recent years
another philosopher, Don Cupitt of Cambridge, has drawn
some of the philosophical and theological flak. D.Z. Phillips
has attempted to show the nonsensicality of a philosophical
investigation into whether, in fact, God exists. Rather, the
question is, first of all, *what kind of reality* God may be said
to have. To condense Phillips' writings into one sentence, his
answer is that God is divinely real. Thus, it makes no sense to
have a concept of God separate from his divinity, as though
the philosopher or theologian could formulate a general
theory about God and then proceed to find detailed evidence
for his existence. To use the technical terms, religious language is expressive and not referential. God, in other words,
is not a name which *refers* to an objective reality. God does
transcend man but we have to pay close attention to the way
the word is used in context to understand the talk of God's
objectivity in a genuine religious sense.

Some would say that D.Z. Phillips is the most significant
British Christian thinker of post-war times. His writings are
subtle and profound and the full force of what he is saying
may not be plainly obvious to some of his readers. However,
there can be no mistaking the message in Don Cupitt's trenchant writings, particularly in his *Taking Leave of God* and
The World to Come. Cupitt's position is not identical to that
of Phillips but he is obviously writing from within Wittgenstein's legacy. Cupitt wants to free Christianity from its
belief in the objective God out there, its theological realism to
use his own terms. If we pay attention to the true context of
religious language, namely, religious spirituality, we see the
irrelevance of the effort to provide a philosophical sub-struc-
ture for faith. Indeed, the pure in heart recognize the demand
for a realistic God as unspiritual. On Cupitt's view, the objective God is the devil.

Cupitt, like Phillips, makes many points which reveal him
to be a thinker of deep spirituality and a man with a profound
grasp of the Christian tradition. Yet, I fear that he has not

been sufficiently radical to avoid an anthropocentric solution to the contemporary dilemmas of religion. Cupitt abolishes the conventional theological God and yet retains what appears to be a conventional understanding of the self. This is particularly obvious in his talk of faith as an act of the will and the spiritual ideal as something which a believer could *attain*. The treasure is contained in a very earthen vessel – an individual who has swallowed the socialized convention of the self who stands over against the world. One of the purposes of the present study is to show that it is just such an understanding of the self which will not bear the revolution in theological thinking. We need a sense of the self deep enough for the incarnation of which Heinrich Zimmer spoke. Alan Watts and Krishnamurti offer us many clues to what this understanding of the self could be. Cupitt used a saying by Meister Eckhart as an epigraph for one of his own books; 'Man's last and highest parting occurs when, for God's sake, he takes leave of God.' In the present context we could rephrase this; 'Man's last and highest parting occurs when, for the Self's sake, he takes leave of the self.' This will hopefully make some sense in the chapters which follow. Like the followers of Wittgenstein, Alan Watts offers, I believe, an interpretation of religious belief 'outside in,' but he does so in a way which avoids the feeling that by doing so we are made prisoners of our own grammar.

PRISONERS OF GRAMMAR?

The last few pages are merely a simple outline of a view which has come into prominence over the past ten years. It has seemed like a massive dose of philosophical fresh air to some people. Religion cannot be judged in the light of a wider, more comprehensive and authoritative context. This is the good news. What about the bad news? Many have felt, as I suggested in the last section, that the bad news overshadows the good. The bad news appears to be that religion's liberation is bought at the price of having only the language, as distinctive as it maybe in its peculiar religious use. To put the matter crudely, God is not some supreme reality who exists whether people think about him or not; 'God' is an expressive term bound up with the way people have found and spoken about possibilities of meaning in their lives. A novelist as perceptive as Isaac Bashevis Singer has voiced what is, I think, the gut-level response of many; 'I have the. . . .feeling today when I try to read the convoluted commentaries of Wittgenstein and his disciples who try to convince themselves and others that all that we lack is a clear definition of words. Give us a dictionary with crystal-clear definitions. . .and the pains of all the martyrs of all times and of all the tortured creatures would become justified forever.'[153] Professional philosophers tend to react less extremely but make the same basic point. Wittgenstein's analysis, they contend, sounds like Feuerbach all over again. The religious realities are being reduced to purely human concerns. Such reactions to Wittgenstein are predictable but they are, I believe, mistaken. In no sense could Wittgenstein be classified as a reductionist in the tradition of Feuerbach.

We are now back with the problem I raised at the close of the second chapter after the discussion of Krishnamurti. Is it meaningful to say that in some contexts not only certain uses are inadequate but that language as such is inadequate? The discussion of this problem has become very technical and I can only refer the reader to fuller accounts at this point.[154] Nevertheless, without all the qualifications which would have to be made in a more detailed exposition, it appears that neither Wittgenstein nor his modern followers allow for the sense that man may be the victim of language. The Wittgensteinians certainly show how human beings are the beneficiaries of language, but is this sufficient? After all, at the heart of Krishnamurti's and Watts' approach is the conviction that language somehow puts us on 'automatic,' that it is itself a reducing valve in some states of consciousness.

There is an ambiguity in Wittgenstein's thought on this

matter when we look over his lifetime's output. We noticed earlier that at one stage he could imagine a religion in which no language was used. However, it is difficult to square this with his later writings. One of his most prolific followers in the philosophy of religion, D.Z. Phillips, probably brings out Wittgenstein's later view most consistently when he comments, 'One cannot have religion without religious discourse'[155] implying that the language we use is inseparable from the experiences described through it. The range of possible experiences goes hand in hand with the range of the possibilities in the language. This raises a very telling question. How would the Wittgensteinian approach analyze a form of religion which had at its heart an alleged direct apprehension of reality outside all language systems? As I have said, Krishnamurti and Alan Watts hold this to be the case as, of course, do many forms of eastern philosophies and religions. Would Wittgenstein's followers be bound to say that what is impossible epistemologically is impossible religiously?

This really brings forward the problem in an acute form. It is put in a clear and provocative way by the great Zen Buddhist scholar D.T. Suzuki. At one stage in his *Essays in Zen Buddhism* (First Series), he discusses the meaning of *yathabhutam* – the contemplation of the world as it is, and refers to what he calls the Buddha's radical empiricism;

> By this I mean that he took life and the world as they were and did not try to read them according to his own interpretation. Theorists may say this is impossible, for we put our subjectivity into every act of perception, and what we call an objective world is really a reconstruction of our innate ideas. Epistemologically this may be so, but all our egoistic thoughts are not read into life and the world is accepted as it is as a mirror reflects a flower as flower and the moon as moon. When therefore I say Buddhism is radical empiricism, this is not to be understood epistemologically but spiritually.[156]

This is a blunt refusal by Suzuki to have his religious position placed in a wider empirical context and judged. The commonsense, western empirical approach that we find in A.J. Ayer and Antony Flew certainly would not constitute such a context for Suzuki. It would not be empirical enough. It would be an expression in philosophical terms of a dominant western world picture, the myth of objective consciousness.[157]

Suzuki is making the same kind of point as Alan Watts and Krishnamurti. They are speaking of a state of consciousness in which the knower-known split, the ego-world gap, is transcended. Knower and known are to be understood in a similar way to which we understand the 'ends' of a rod. The 'ends' of a rod are geometrical imaginations like mathematical points. There is no sense in which the ends 'meet' in something we call a rod. They are terms not entities just as we talk of north and south on a sphere. Knower and known are points on the knowing ball.

The last few pages should have shown that we need to have reservations about some aspects of the Wittgensteinian analysis. Nevertheless, it seems to me to be the most open minded approach available in contemporary philosophy to give the kind of thinking we find in Watts and company a toehold in the western debates. It provides, in other words, a philosophical context for considering two fundamentally different world pictures without the one being assimilated to the other. Let me conclude this chapter with a specific example of what I mean. In an earlier study[158] I mentioned a radio talk given some years ago by Marghanita Laski in which she said that she regarded 'faith' as a vice because it was living 'as if.' She preferred to live with what 'is.' What *is*, presumably, is what is ordinary and obvious. Religious faith is 'what is as if' and a doubtful intrusion into everyday paramount reality. In her technical study, *Ecstasy*, she says that 'Ecstasy is...applied to experiences that are different in seeming to lie outside the normal course of events.'[159] We find a very different world picture in Alan Watts' exposition of the Hindu tradition visually expressed in the temple of Konarak;

It is not, today, either a respectable or popular notion that to be aware of reality is ecstasy. We speak, rather, of grim realities, harsh truths, and hard facts, and ecstasy is – by and large – considered primitive, disreputable, subhuman, irrational, and close to madness. There is, indeed, no place or occasion for ecstasy in a world of mere objects. . . . In its many forms and moods, ecstasy is life itself. The very word *ek-stasis* means to stand outside, to be liberated from the bondage of oneself – the conceptual ego, personality, and role-player that one is supposed to be. In ecstasy one is no longer an object a thing or being – alone and separate from the total energy of the world. The ecstatic is beyond the pale of a classified, name-formed, and regimented society where everyone must identify himself with a fixed role.[160]

There is a very forceful expression of belief in 'a world of mere objects' in Bertrand Russell's book, *The Scientific Outlook*. Russell would probably have classified Watts' view as 'monism.' This, however, is to miss the point. Monism is itself a dualistic word. Leaving this aside consider this extract from Russell's book;

The most fundamental of my intellectual beliefs is that (monism) is rubbish. I think the universe is all spots and jumps, without unity, without continuity, without coherence or orderliness, or any of the other properties that governesses love.[161]

It is very obvious that the notion of ecstasy would mean very different things to Laski and Russell on the one hand and Watts on the other. For Watts, ecstasy is ruled out by definition where the world is thought to be made up of objects. The world that Watts speaks about is not the same as Russell's. If both speak about ecstasy they are not providing two different uses of the *same* notion. To use a way of speaking found earlier in this chapter; they use the same *words* but speak a different *language*. It is exactly this kind of distinction which Wittgenstein's approach helps us to understand. We can make the point a little more picturesquely by recalling R.H. Blyth's reply to his students when they asked him whether he believed in God. He said, 'If you don't, I do. If you do, I don't.' The God believed in by the faithful is not the God doubted by the sceptic.

THE FIRST PRINCIPLE

The contrast between Watts and Russell could scarcely be greater. The whole thrust of Watts' writings is against the primacy of what he sometimes called the rusty beer can view of reality, the world experienced as a collection of objects scrubbed clean of mystery. It is presumably because Russell experienced the world as 'all spots and jumps' that he could write books with such aggressive sounding titles as *The Conquest of Nature*. The experience of the world which seems to underly Russell's way of speaking is still, I would say, at the heart of western commonsense. It is not really surprising that the kind of consciousness of which Watts' speaks should be misunderstood or merely classified as muddled. This is intensified when we learn that we cannot conceptualize the transformed state of consciousness. On Watts' view, the multiple differentiations of the universe have a basis but there is no word for it. We can, in other words, have no idea of the non-distinction. We may feel it but not name it. We notice and, therefore, talk about particular 'grasps' of perception but we are often oblivious to our underlying consciousness. It is a *constant* and we ignore it. We notice white chalk marks and ignore the black background; we notice clouds and ignore the blue sky; we notice thoughts in the mind and ignore consciousness.

The issue here recalls a Zen story. There is no concept 'God,' as such, in Zen Buddhism. Instead, there is a rough equivalent, 'the first principle.' A student once asked; 'Master, what is the first principle?' and received the reply; 'If I were to tell you, it would become the second principle.'

All the debates about the truth of religion are, of necessity on the level of second principle. There is a second principle precisely because there is a first principle – which can never be named. It can be felt and experienced in a transformed state of consciousness. This, at least, is the claim which I am considering here.

5 Transcending the grammar

THERE IS A FAMOUS passage in Wittgenstein's early book, the *Tractatus*, which is strangely close to the kind of view expressed in many of Alan Watts' writings. Wittgenstein refers to the state where the problems of life vanish;

> We feel that even if *all possible* scientific questions be answered, the problems of life have still not been touched at all. Of course there is then no question left, and just this is the answer. The solution of the problem of life is seen in the vanishing of this problem.[162]

Wittgenstein comes to this position through philosophical reflection. Watts comes to a similar point in a certain state of consciousness. He expresses it in the following way;

> All the problems vanish when you are in the non verbal dimension of consciousness. Theology, philosophy and metaphysics as we ordinarily talk about them cease to be urgent problems. You see the answers to all the questions that theologians and metaphysicians ask and you see why their questions are absurd.[163]

Watts seems to be talking here of what Aldous Huxley called a 'grammar – transcending experience'; 'The enlightened individual goes beyond grammar...and is, so to speak, *after* the rise of language; he lives in the language and then goes beyond it.'[164] Huxley would have been the first to add that such a person goes on using language. His comments here point to distinction evident in Watts' writings which is very relevant to the main issues of this book. The mode of consciousness *changes the status of the language*.

In his *Behold the Spirit* Watts distinguishes two attitudes to the function of language among religious believers which resembles the distinction between the two attitudes towards language which applies in ordinary circumstances:

> For those who *cannot* at present understand anything beyond forms, it is a way of speeding up and intensifying the attempt to possess God until they become quite convinced by experience that he cannot be possessed. In addition, it imparts a symbolic, analogical knowledge of God which . . . gives them courage to venture into the Reality beyond symbols. For those who *can* go beyond forms, it is a way not of getting but of expressing, of making incarnate and concrete, their spiritual realization and its effects. It is language and grammar at the disposal of inner meaning.[165]

Watts thinks that it is possible to distinguish between two uses of language, one operating at a more profound level than the other. The more superficial use is that language used by believers who feel it as an instrument groping towards a reality external to them and for which they long. The second and more profound use is that of language as *itself* an expression of the state of realization. It is not a hand reaching to touch a hair; it is a hair growing from the head. The task of bringing words back from their metaphysical use to their true home can now be seen in a different light. It is a deepening process, setting words in their most profound context. This setting is the experience of realization and not, to quote Watts, the psychoanalytical garbage can. The supreme experience is now consciousness where life is truly alive;

When the dead man talks, he gives us the facts; he tells us all and says nothing. But when the living man talks, he gives us poetry and myth.... He gives us a word...not from the psychoanalytical garbage can, but from the living world which is not to be remembered, of which no trace can be found in history, in the record of facts, because it is not yet dead.... Thus poetry and myth are accounts of the real world which *is*, as distinct from the dead world which *was*, and therefore *will* be.'[166]

Let me try to spell out the issues here. There are two levels to be distinguished. The first is that where experience is in some sense at the disposal of the language and the grammar. For those on this level of experience, the realities expressed in the language are external realities. God, for example, is felt to be a supreme reality to which the language is pointing. Although they may not realise it, the language is giving them courage at this stage to, perhaps, go further to a deeper stage where the language and symbols do not 'arrive' at a reality but have their status changed into *expressions* of the realized state. At this second level the language and grammar is at the disposal of inner meaning. This is the true home of the words. Here they express and embody a reality rather than point to it. So understood, the language expresses the wider and deeper sense of identity of which Watts speaks. If the words *point* at all it is to the centre of ourselves, that is the deep and universal centre not the 'little old me,' the ego. As I have said more than once, this deepened sense of identity does not strictly speaking have a language. Yet men and women have tried to put it into words, to eff the ineffable and unscrew the inscrewtable. And why not? Language also is part of the Tao. However, such language is misunderstood when it is thought to point to realities which require some sort of belief. The language most expressive of the experience under discussion is mythological and poetic in form. In his study, *The Two*

Element Books Ltd

Publishers and Distributors

I would like to be placed on the Element Books Mailing List and to receive the Element Books Catalogue.

Name (*Block Capitals*) ....

Address ....

....

....

Country ....

ELEMENT BOOKS LTD.
23 ALL SAINTS VILLAS ROAD
CHELTENHAM
GLOUCESTERSHIRE
GL52 2HB

Hands of God, Watts distinguishes between factual and mythological language: 'Factual language dissects and disintegrates experience into categories and oppositions that cannot be resolved.'[167] We could say, as Watts himself does in a different study, that 'all language is geared to the realm of relativity,'[168] but that factual or referential language is particularly so. Where religious language is interpreted referentially it points away from the place where it has its true home. On the other hand, mythological language is 'integrative'; 'the language of the image is *organic* language.'[169] Watts quotes Coomaraswamy with approval; 'myth embodies the nearest approach to absolute truth that can be stated in words.'[170] Such a language grows from the depths and needs to be related to the depths to be understood. Myths do, of course, lose their grip in certain culturally determined circumstances. As Wittgenstein would say about pictures; when they die something dies with them that cannot be revived by willpower or replaced by intellectually generated alternatives. It is tempting for theologians to try to reinstate beliefs which have lost their power. Watts, like Wittgenstein's followers, was critical of these efforts. Such attempts at reinstatement were imitations and the results inevitably sound hollow.[171]

It may be worthwhile at this point to relate the two level distinction in Watts' writings to some aspects of Wittgenstein's thought discussed in the previous chapter. To adopt Wittgenstein's terms; an outsider may know the surface grammar of religious belief and yet not understand its depth grammar. Where there is only a surface understanding the religious words easily go astray into foreign fields of discourse and need to be brought back to their true, 'everyday' home. So far in this chapter I have used Watts' thinking to draw yet another surface-depth distinction *within* the sphere of religion itself. This distinction is to be understood in terms of states or qualities of consciousness. At the surface level of the religious life, the words do indeed appear to *point to* external realities. At a deeper level they are *themselves* expressions of a state of realization. Their status, as words, is changed. There are a few comments written by Wittgenstein in a notebook of 1937 (published as *Culture and Value*; Oxford: Blackwell, 1980) which come near to the distinction I am making here:

> In religion every level of devoutness must have its appropriate form of expression which has no sense at a lower level. This doctrine, which means something at a higher level, is null and void for someone who is still at the lower level; he *can* only understand it *wrongly* and so these words are *not* valid for such a person.

In the context of the present discussion I would substitute 'level of consciousness' for Wittgenstein's 'level of devoutness.' Wittgenstein, in fact, goes on to provide an example and modestly puts himself on the lower level:

> For instance, at my level the Pauline doctrine of predestination is ugly nonsense, irreligiousness. Hence it is not suitable for me, since the only use I could make of the picture I am offered would be a wrong one. If it is a good and godly picture, then it is for someone at a quite different level, who must use it in his life in a way completely different from anything that would be possible for me. (p.32)

In his published writings Wittgenstein had much more to say about the sense of distinguishing between belief and unbelief rather than about levels of understanding within the religious life itself. Without himself being a religious person in any narrowly doctrinal sense, he had a profound grasp of the ways in which the religious pictures are eroded by changes in language and culture.

What consequences, we may ask, follow from circumstances where the analogies of religion are under cultural pressures of a severe kind? Many commentators would say that we are living through such a time. Let me answer this question from the point of view I have developed from Watts' writings. The circumstances will be viewed differently by people occupying the different levels we distinguished earlier. Those for whom the language is understood referentially, who are in some way at the disposal of language and grammar, will be discouraged. A meaningful referential language exists, after all, to give them courage. Where a language understood in this way becomes feeble and tired, the realities it once clearly pointed to appear as doubtful entities. There is then a search on the part of the theologians for more adequate concepts to bring into clearer focus the objects of belief. This is a very common understanding of the present dilemma of religion and the standardized task of the theologian.

What of those on the second level? A few pages earlier I used Aldous Huxley's term 'grammar – transcending experience' to describe part of the transformed sense of identity which is central to Watts' thought. In a deep and important sense, those at the second level are untouched by the pressures to which the religious analogies are subjected. As I have said, language is part of the Tao. A culture and its language may develop to a point where it seems inimical to religion, but it cannot avoid the Tao. The language is still itself a gesture. A person may lament the fact that a language has developed in such a way as to make the analogies barren. His sensibilities may be depressed by this. As Watts observed; 'As water seeks the course of least resistance, so the emotions clothe themselves in the symbols that lie most readily to hand.'[172] The water flows freely but it follows the form of the terrain. To adapt the metaphor slightly, the cultural terrain may restrict the way in which the religious analogies are expressed and depress the emotions of the people concerned. Nevertheless, as Watts comments in the same essay; 'how I *feel*, whether the actual sensation of freedom and clarity is present or not, is not the point – for, again, to feel heavy or restricted is also IT.'[173] To put the matter simply, the central reality is only affected by the changes and chances of a developing language and culture in terms of the analogies which give it expression.

ANALYZING ECSTASY

In several parts of the discussion so far many readers will have detected the far off rumblings of a boulder which has rolled progressively nearer and which is now about to arrive in the form of a blunt question. What *sense* is there in speaking of an experience which supposedly 'transcends grammar'? The late Paul Tillich once challenged a philosopher to attend his lectures and raise his finger if he heard something which appeared to be philosophically meaningless. Every limb on the bodies of most contemporary western philosophers would twitch at the idea of a grammar transcending experience. It seems to preclude, by definition, any language *about* it. Even if we grant, for the sake of argument, the non-verbal state of consciousness of which Watts speaks, is it even *possible* for us simply to look and experience what is there? The logical philosophers have demonstrated, to their own satisfaction at least, that we cannot say anything about everything in any meaningful sense. The theologians have found many different ways of saying that everything is everything but that is all they amount to. So goes the linguistic critique. However, a similar point has been made in many other fields; aesthetics, psychology, anthropology. We can no more *feel* about everything than we can say anything about everything. Since all our senses are selective, it follows that we experience as well as think by contrast. As George Steiner observed, we are all neo-Kantians now;[174] 'Human perception and activity, even at levels which seem most spontaneous, most "natural," are now thought to be highly conventionalized. We feel, we see, we communicate our sense of an exterior world not in some inevitable organic or immediate way, but through specialized processes of expectation and selection.'[175] In other words, our experience of reality is determined by certain selective categories and stylised codes of language. What was implicit in Kant's theory of knowledge is now openly and fully realised in every dimension of man's life. Numerous examples could be given. The writings of the art historian, E.H. Gombrich, illustrate the point very well. Constable never saw a field, for example, simply and naturally as it was. His view was determined by stylistic expectations of what to look for.

There is no reason to think that Watts and Krishnamurti would disagree with any of this. One of their major arguments, after all, is that we are put onto 'automatic' by categories of thought and systems of language. Their point is that there is a state of consciousness in which this 'determined' state is transcended. Let me take as a point of departure here a passage from Nelson Goodman's *Languages of Art* on the subject of the 'thinking eye';

> There is no innocent eye. The eye comes always ancient to its work. Not only how but what it sees is regulated by need and prejudice. It selects, rejects, organizes, discriminates, associates, classifies, analyses, constructs. It does not so much mirror as take and make.... Nothing is seen nakedly or naked.'[176]

The passage begs the whole question of the identity of that which 'takes and makes.' Whatever it is, it is incapable, according to Goodman, of reflecting simply what is there. By contrast, the Buddhist and Taoist traditions frequently speak of the true self as a mirror reflecting what is there and being unaffected at the deepest level. A mirror accepts anything and does not discriminate between one sight and another. It reflects flowers and dung alike. As Chuang-tzu remarks; 'It grasps nothing, it refuses nothing. It receives but does not keep; therefore, it is never stained. It has no colour; therefore, it reflects all colours.'[177] We may reply, of course, that we are talking about the mind and not a mirror. If the mind is a mirror it is selective or flawed in a way which distorts what is there. Bankei admits this; 'Remember that all you see and hear is reflected in the Buddha-mind and influenced by what was previously seen and heard.'[178] The Buddha-mind contains that which 'takes and makes,' thoughts and abstractions from memory. But, for Bankei, these are illusory. He continues; 'Needless to say, thoughts are not entities. If you permit them to rise and reflect themselves, or cease altogether, as they are prone to do – if you do not worry about them, you will never go astray. . . . You will remain undisturbed.'[179]

As we have seen throughout this study, much of Watts' output is devoted to exploring the meaning of the 'You' in the last sentence. The 'you' which is easily disturbed is the ego, an abstraction from memory, an idea we have of ourselves. But that is all it is; a social convention. It has not reality in the sense that, say, the pituitary gland has. We are, obviously, aware of something we feel to be ourselves. We feel ourselves to be the subject of the events that make up our lives. Watts is asking us to see this feeling of self and what we experience as other as poles in a single process. What I see, make and take, is as much me as what I identify as my inner being. If the discursive intellect imagines itself as an isolated entity it will naturally find insuperable difficulties in talking about a 'grammar-transcending' experience and a non verbal state of consciousness. If I realize that this scanning consciousness is merely a conventional habit, I also realize that *what* I see is so central to my experience that it can never become an object. Not to realize this may mean that I need to search for it. To do so means that I lose the sense of it. On the other hand, I may realize my essential identity with everything else and want to talk about it. However, the only way I can do so is by using the very dualistic language which encourages the sense of the I's separate reality.

Alan Watts was well aware of the kind of critical pressures, philosophical and otherwise, which have been directed to those who speak of a transformed state of consciousness. He tried in some of his writings to expose the fact that the linguistic, technical philosopher had an unexamined philosophical subconscious, a sense of reality which was the assumed background of all his thinking. If the philosopher persisted in this state of mind, there was little chance that he would be satisfied by statements about the transformed state. About the best one could do, accepting the philosopher's word game, was to say something like the following; 'All knowledge is a recognition of the mutual relations between sense-experiences and/or things and events' and 'All things are known by their differences from and likenesses to each other.'[180] This is hardly likely, however, to satisfy the hard-line philosopher. The inherent impossibility of maintaining the Watts' position and complying with the philosopher's criteria are shown very well in a passage from A.J. Ayer's *Language, Truth and Logic*. This statement is almost forty years old, yet the sense of reality it assumes is still presupposed in many modern debates;

> We do not deny *a priori* that the mystic is able to discover truths by his own special methods. We wait to hear what are the propositions which embody his discoveries, in order to see whether they are verified or confuted by our empirical observations.[181]

The point is that the so-called mystic has to express his 'discoveries' in a language mutually acceptable to and understandable by both mystic and sceptical philosopher. As Ayer continues; 'It is no use his saying that he has apprehended facts but is unable to express them. For we know that if he really had acquired any information, he would be able to express it.'[182] Consider Watts' position in the light of this comment. He has advocated the possibility of a non-verbal, non-conceptual state of consciousness in which we may be aware of all the mutual interdependencies of processes which are separated and distinguished by words. The language separates the processes only conventionally. How is Watts to say so when the very act of *saying* inherits this very convention, that existence is a collection of bits and pieces? As he muses in his exposition of the philosophy built into the temple at Konarak; 'modern logical and linguistic philosophy is correct in its criticism of traditional Western metaphysics; yet individual philosophers of this school seldom, if ever, go into that silence beyond the exhaustion of language where they might have a metaphysical experience instead of an idea.'[183] When the technical philosopher asks for the meaning of such statements as, 'We are living in an eternal now,' he is asking for another set of signs, a construct of more words; 'What *is* meaning is distinct from what *has* meaning never enters into his game.'[184]

Ultimately, the technical philosopher and the person who shares the kind of view we find in Watts' writings must go their separate ways. Neither wishes to play the other's game. Watts' position does not allow for the possibility of there being a wider philosophical context in which his view may be set and judged by the canons of western academic philosophy. This is a view which is generally supported by Wittgenstein, as we have seen. The technical philosopher is analyzing a position which is, to say the very least, one which includes a sense of identity, of 'I,' quite different from that of his own. It would be misleading, however, to think that the two sides can henceforth only send acrimonious 'reminders' to each other. Indeed, Watts thinks that logical philosophy has made an important contribution to the clarification of the kind of position he has put forward. Its positive contribution has, unfortunately been obscured by the emotional bias of some of its exponents.[185] Its criticism of religious statements as conveying information about 'transcendental objects' is perfectly justified. Watts notes that oriental philosophy has never seriously thought that metaphysical statements convey positive information about 'reality' as though it were an object of knowledge. They are intended more for correcting a process whereby human beings frustrate themselves with unreal problems. Logical philosophy has performed a similar function except that few western philosophers would agree with the oriental philosopher about the nature of the 'Reality' which is seen when unreality has been removed. Up to a point, logical philosophy is a much needed western technique of negation if it frees us from the illusion that 'Reality' may be defined and somehow possessed by words. This same philosophy has been lethal, of course, for that tradition of theological thinking which has spoken of God or ultimate reality as having specific properties.

Before moving into the final sections of this chapter it may be useful to say in a few sentences just how far Watts' position may be verified as being true, fitting the facts, or however we may wish to put it. The situation seems to be this. Where religious people make assertions about doubtful transcendental entities they do have cause to be doubted. They may nonetheless 'believe' in face of the evidence but this is not the kind of religious stance that impresses Watts. Where there is belief there is always the nagging feeling of doubt. The state of transformed identity, of being at one with God in religious terms, cannot be set into a neutral context where it may be checked and verified as the truth. For Watts, as for Wittgenstein, truth is a context – dependent notion: 'The meaning of the assertion is the experience itself. Outside that state of consciousness it has no meaning.'[186] Again, 'Debates as to whether this vision is or is not "true" seem as pointless as asking whether my sensation of green is just the same as yours.'[187]

WHO DO THE THEOLOGIANS THINK THEY ARE?

This question is not at all facetious. It's as important to ask *who* is writing the theology as to wonder *who* is asking the question. Most books on theology are clarifications, as is almost any book, of the author's own state of mind however much they may appear to be written for a wider public. Their own understanding of themselves is obviously crucial to the content to the resulting theology. If he or she is a tortured intellectual writing from within a sceptical milieu, it will show. And it does. Take, for example, the recent debates centering around the books by the Cambridge philosopher of religion Don Cupitt.[188] Cupitt is obviously a man who wants to be ruthlessly honest with himself; 'there must be no more pixie dust.' Two other British theologians with a refreshingly honest approach to their own subject and their own souls are John Hick and Michael Goulder. I recently witnessed a debate in which they defended, respectively, belief in God and the position of the unbeliever. Their arguments where subsequently published as *Why Believe in God?* As always their honesty and lucidity were very impressive but the question which arose in my mind was one which always arises when I read Don Cupitt's books. Why do theologians and philosophers have such a narrow range of options in terms of personal identity? The theological case always, it seems, needs to be made in terms of the conventional western view of the self. Here is a passage by John Hick:

> The fundamental question concerning religious language is whether it *only* expresses certain human states of mind or whether it *also* points, even though always with finite symbols, to an ultimate Reality which is limitlessly more beingful and more valuable than our little human egos. If religious language is *only* expressive, and does not refer to a divine Reality beyond us, then the God of which it ostensibly speaks is a figment of our imaginations.[189]

Why should the possibilities for religious language be restricted to two? Why should religious language *either* refer to an external Reality *or* be expressive of merely human concerns? It is just such an understanding of the alternatives available that is challenged by Watts' thought. His teachings offer a different way through.

If the fundamental religious experience were seen as a form of realization in Watts' terms, then human consciousness and the language which gives it expression is a particular mode *itself* of the ultimate Reality which is essentially identical to the ground of the whole universe. From this standpoint the task of the theologians and theology is seen in a quite different light. Theologians will not torture themselves in an effort to find more adequate images of God or refine those concepts they already have. They will be, rather, celebrating a new feeling of what it is to be 'I.'[190] In his *Nature, Man and Woman*, Watts comments that it is largely in the image of the superficial self that God has been conceived. It is God conceived in the image of severed consciousness. Because we restrict the self to the contents of conscious attention we feel that there are whole areas 'outside' of us. Hence, God is felt to be supremely 'other,' a reality in complete creative control, the meaning of all things being transparently clear to him. Watts wonders whether this is, in fact, what we westerners would really like ourselves to be; 'a person in total control of himself, analyzed to the ultimate depths of his own unconscious, understood and explained to the last atom of his brain, and to this extent completely mechanized.'[191]

The God based on the model of severed consciousness has proved a real problem. If theologians accept the conventional split between self and other, the knower and the known, there is no reason why they should not lumber themselves with all the other conventional distinctions as well. By and large this is what has happened. God has been conceived to have the same kind of objective, intractable reality which we think of when we talk of 'hard facts.' There is a difference, albeit the most important one. This is the basic reason why there has been so much conflict between science and religion. They can only disagree if they are speaking the same language. Scientists rely on the conventional distinctions of fact, event, etc. That is their game. Theologians join in the game and cannot possibly win. There is no way in which he can demonstrate the reality of God as a separate, factual entity. He is using a language inappropriate to the subject matter.

Many readers may feel that all this is very well, but that there is a rather obvious question that needs, indeed, begs to be answered. *Why* should anyone see his or her own deepest nature as at one with and an expression of the ultimate reality of the universe? Even if they do, is not this still a *belief*, the very thing that Watts and company scorn? It is a belief, of course, if that is the only thing we can manage. To recall the distinction between the two understandings of language which I mentioned at the beginning of this chapter; this is the permanent situation for those at the first level. They understand the language as something *pointing to* an external reality in which they firmly believe. The language and belief give them intellectual courage. It is this level that theologians habitually address their thoughts to. There is, however, as Watts is at pains to show, a different and further possibility, a state of realization. Readers would have to consult the writings of Watts themselves, as well, of course, as the religious and philosophical traditions to have detailed accounts of this state. I can only make an impossibly brief summary here and say realization is not the discovery of new or amazing facts. It is more to do with the removal of unreality. This process may sound very negative, as when we say that concepts must be abandoned. The point is, however, that this is meant to reveal that what is empty is not reality itself but all that seems to block its light. Those who experience the non verbal dimension of consciousness see why their vision of reality is truly ineffable. They do not have a true *conception* of what is really going on in a way that could be stated were they but lucid enough. Alan Watts puts it in this way;

> In trying to escape convention and the barriers that words create between you and reality, you may choose to renounce your identity, in effect saying "Now the game is over. Let's find out what lay behind it. What is really going on?"
>
> Be very careful that the next passing swami does

not sell you still another institutionalized version
of the real world. For instance, the notion that
when you are awakened all differentiations will
vanish is a conventional view of the universe.[192]

This could sound like the ultimate put-down to some
people. After all, isn't the whole point that we should see that
all differentiations vanish? To say this, however, is to miss
the point. The conception of a non-dual universe is just
another conception. Let me adapt one of Wittgenstein's
images and put it this way. The process of awakening is like
trying to open a safe with a combination lock. Each little
denial of a concept or word – not that, not that – each small
adjustment of the dials, seems to achieve nothing. Only when
all is in place (or should we say out of the way?) does the door
open.

THE MENU AND THE MEAL

Before moving on to more specific matters in the final
chapters, I want to take up a difficulty which I mentioned in
the course of discussing Krishnamurti. To live totally in the
present, to feel that there is nothing in life to be attained
which is not already here, may be seen as the atomization of
life into point instants, a succession of senseless present
moments. This is an impression very easily gained from
Krishnamurti's writings. If we supplement the latter with
Alan Watts', we can see how this reaction is a misunderstanding.

If we suspend thought, then the abstractions of past and
future disappear like phantoms. If we simply look and see,
without symbolizing to ourselves, we realize that there is just
this present moment. This realization, however, need not
destroy what we could call the sense of life. In this now
moment we are aware of what Buddhists call 'suchness.'
There is just this happening now. As the Zen thinker, Dogen,
said, the firewood does not *become* ashes; the spring does not

become the summer. There is the firewood and there are the ashes. Yet in the winter we can see the *traces* of the spring; in the spring we can see the *traces* of summer. We see a tree and infer that there was a seed; we see tracks on the sand and infer there was a bird. The past and the future are contained in the present. Although there is just the present moment, it contains within itself a whole universe of meaning. There is no incompatibility about living totally in the present and dealing with the past and future. Our memories and expectations are always in the present. Nevertheless, we may enjoy the continuities of remembering the past and making plans for the future. Once we have seen the illusion of past and future we may live totally in the present and enjoy the illusion.

In addition to this something also needs to be added about another possible misunderstanding of Krishnamurti's teaching. He urges us to live free of thought. When we read Mao Tse-Tung's Red Book saying that 'It is essential to have a furrowed brow to think,' Krishnamurti's offer seems positively attractive. Nevertheless, living without thinking seems to rule out the possibility of true spontaneity in thinking about thinking. This, again, would be a misunderstanding. As we saw in the first chapter, thinking may well make us miss the feast. We intellectualize the moment and eat the menu instead of the meal. Yet it has to be said that words have their own reality just as much as clouds and flowers. There is nothing unnatural in the world. Thoughts about thoughts are themselves realities in their own way. They do, of course, seduce us away from the present moment experience, but they need not do so. If we do not experience a word or thought as a block, there is no reason why we should not be spontaneously in the present moment when we are thinking about thinking. The intellectual is not automatically destined to starve to death by arriving late for the feast.

Another reason why I have mentioned this here is to provide a context for the next chapter which looks at Christian beliefs in particular. In traditional Christian thought God has been conceived as being so 'other' than us, that to talk about being *at one* with his reality sounds like an extreme form of megalomania. It does not sound so mad to say that one lives totally in the present moment, yet it does, I believe, amount to much the same thing. If a person lives by the Christian analogy, this is God's world and to be totally alive and sensitive in the present is to realize and celebrate this reality. It does not follow that a person should abandon his or her Christian identity. It does mean, however, that they do not interpret the traditional doctrines out of a sense of duty. Doctrines and beliefs can put us on 'automatic' and out of a consciousness of the present just as any thought may do. It is true that Christianity, along with Judaism, has been pre-eminently the religion of time. Nevertheless, if we do come to see the conventional and illusory nature of time, Christianity may come alive in a quite unimagined way. It may, incidently, reveal to us also that if we believe in time we do not have any. In the West we have largely been hypnotized into a state of consciousness consisting almost entirely of a massive causative past and an ever absorbing future. Our awareness of the present is infinitesimal, swamped by memory and expectation. Christianity seems to fit this pattern. It is ever hopeful for a future on the basis of an event in the ancient world. The next chapter will look at the possibility of interpreting the Christ event radically so that its antiquity lies not in a backward look but in the realization of a vast depth in the present. The incarnation would then mean that the truth lies in the deep centre of this flesh now. This may be what Heinrich Zimmer had in mind in the words quoted at the close of the introduction. The Christian understanding of incarnation for our time may have to be understood in terms radically at odds with the versions found in standardized doctrine. It may amount to a complete reversal of the traditional view. God *becomes* man – not one man but any person – through a transformation of consciousness when people 'empty' themselves. The division between God and humanity is then not that between radically distinct divine and human spheres. It is the division between the liberated and benighted states of consciousness. Jesus empties himself and becomes divine. This need not alter the devotional place Jesus has in the hearts of Christians. Like the avatars in the Indian tradition he may be revered as someone who was *born* liberated and did not need to *attain* it. Perhaps this is the meaning of the virgin birth for those at the crossroads, where the modern mind crosses the path of ancient tradition. But this is to anticipate the next chapter.

6   *Christian consciousness*

READERS WHO HAVE SOME knowledge of the Christian religion may be wondering how this whole discussion affects
the way they think of the traditional doctrines and beliefs.
Similarly, readers who are influenced by no particular
religious tradition may be asking what it all amounts to in
specific terms. I shall discuss these two questions respectively
in this chapter and the one which follows.

I mentioned earlier how consciousness in the Taoist and
Buddhist traditions has been compared to a mirror. Transformed or enlightened consciousness does not cling to experiences just as a mirror does not cling to the images it reflects.
The mirror is always clear of previously reflected images. It
reveals what is there free of all opinions about what should be
there. Is it possible to interpret the Christian experience in
terms of such states of consciousness? After all, some will say,
Christianity has definite ideas about what is there to be seen.
There is truth in this. Traditionally at least, the Christian
mind does seem to be more like a photographic plate than a
mirror. It has a definite image on the sensitive film and sees
the world through it. This metaphor only seems appropriate,
however, because of the tendency of Christian doctrines to
put us on 'automatic' and experience the moment in terms of
the dead image of the 'known.' In the sections which follow I
shall attempt to point towards a different possibility. I shall
discuss, briefly, the themes of salvation, creation, evil,
forgiveness and spirituality. I begin, however, with the
central issue of Christ.

THE CHRISTOLOGY OF ORDINARY HUMAN BEINGS

Alan Watts is critical of theology at many points but his criticism is most severe towards its treatment of the historical character of belief. The following comment is very characteristic; 'Christianity began to die in the moment when theologians began to treat the divine story as history — when they mistook the story of God, of the Creation, and the Fall for a record of facts in the historical past.'[193] Many believers would accede to the implications of this remark so far as the Creation and Fall are concerned. They would balk, however, at the suggestion that the person and the career of Jesus should be treated in the same way. The whole case for Christianity, they would say, rests on the 'scandal of particularity.' That is, God revealed himself supremely once in a real human life, that of Jesus of Nazareth. Watts calls this the 'historical abnormality' theory. According to this, the incarnation is not only confined to the 'dead' past but is further confined to one unique individual. The demythologized 'Jesus of history' is no more profound. He becomes a prophet urging us to changes in behaviour rather than in transformations of consciousness.

It is true that the person of Jesus has attracted the devotion of millions. Nevertheless, the deep appeal of Christianity can hardly be to his ethical teachings alone or to his personality, even if it were possible to know about these with certainty. The picture of Jesus that comes through the New Testament is, for many others, angular and unattractive. D.T. Suzuki has an interesting essay on crucifixion and enlightenment in which he discusses the psychological division between East and West in the light of the 'vertical' death of Christ and the 'horizontal' death of the Buddha.'[194] Many others have drawn attention to the contrast between the beatific Buddha and the grimacing saviour but Suzuki observes that, to the oriental mind, the sight of the helpless, crucified Jesus on the cross is almost unbearable. The vertical cross suggests combativeness and agitation. By contrast, the reclining, horizontal Buddha suggests broad-mindedness, peace and tolerance. Similarly, the sitting meditative Buddha, with centre of gravity in the loins, implies serenity and compassion. Suzuki concludes that the starkly contrasting images reflect a profound gap between Buddhism and Christianity which in turn reflects their respective understanding of the nature of the self. Crucifixion is unnecessary from the Buddhist viewpoint because there is no 'self' to be crucified.

Suzuki was a profound thinker and his comments about the separative and aggressive symbolism at the heart of the Christian faith are hardly superficial. It is, no doubt, difficult for western Christians to imagine just how ego-centred their religion may appear to a Buddhist. Yet, I would say, Christianity has aspects which are open to a more profound interpretation than that found in popular Christian under-standing and which is the object of Suzuki's criticism. In other writings, in fact, Suzuki has drawn attention to areas in which Christianity and Buddhism are very close. In a talk, 'Christianity and Buddhism' (published in *The Eastern Buddhist*, Autumn 1983), Suzuki draws a parallel between truth, freedom and enlightenment; 'Christians say "the truth shall make us free"; according to Buddhism enlightenment frees us. So Christian "truth" is Buddhist "enlightenment," we might say'(p.3). Nevertheless, in the same talk, he repeats the question raised above. He puts the question in terms remarkably reminiscent of the language of existentialist theologians; 'Why were the three days necessary? This is where Buddhism differs from Christianity. Buddhism would say crucifixion *means* resurrection; not crucifixion followed by resurrection. Crucifixion is itself resurrection'(p.6).

Superficially at least Christianity and Buddhism do seem to be divided by the differing estimates of the status of their respective founders, Jesus of Nazareth and Siddhartha Gautama. Everyone, it seems, is a Buddha but only one is the Christ. Gautama was a remarkable man who realized he was Buddha, awakened. This is something all people may become or, indeed, *are* in their essential nature. Anyone can be just as much a Buddha as the Buddha was. Jesus is regarded as unique, the Christ, someone whom all people may *imitate*. Buddhahood is a universal possibility, a supreme realization in the context of the total range of human experience. Gautama himself was not unique in the sense that his Buddhahood was not exclusive to his person. Jesus, however, is traditionally thought to be one of a kind. His status as Christ is inseparable from his person, Jesus of Nazareth. The history of Christianity is littered with complicated arguments, often bitter, about exactly how he could be *both* in a unique sense. The debates still rage. The most recent skirmishes have centred on the mythological nature, or otherwise, of the incarnation. It may be worthwhile to look at the issue in a different way. Gautama the person is separable from his buddhistic realization. Why should we not talk in similar way about Jesus and his consciousness as the Christ? Christ consciousness, the experience of oneness with the divine ground of the universe, would be seen as a universal possibility open to all people. Jesus of Nazareth realized this in a startling way, but such a state of consciousness need not necessarily be realizable solely through the *person* of Jesus. People may experience this state through other channels. It is true that the Jesus of the gospels often appears to make exclusive claims about himself – 'No one comes to the Father except by me,' and so on. The 'me,' however, could be interpreted, in the context of the present study, as referring to the unitive, 'Christ' state of consciousness rather than to the particular person who uttered the words.

This suggestion does not rule out the possibility of devotion to Jesus as a person. In one sense Christianity itself may be seen as a form of bhakti or devotional yoga. Indeed, the life and teachings of Jesus could be regarded as a form of yoga. Yoga means union, the opposite of alienation, in sociological terms, or 'separateness,' in Buddhist terms. A person's yoga is his or her way of answering the questions 'Who am I?' and 'Where do I belong?' Jesus is reported to have said that his yoke was easy. In the present context this may be taken to mean that his yoga or means of union was easy. Thus, union with God is not something to be *achieved*. It is simply to realize what is *already* the case. There is no mountain separating us from God. Buddhists, incidently, have a vivid mountain image illustrating the immensity of the task facing someone who imagines that realization will come in time through sheer effort. Imagine a mountain of solid granite six miles high, six miles wide and six miles long. Once every one hundred years a bird flies past and brushes the mountain with a silk scarf. How long will it take to wear down the mountain? Jesus also spoke of faith using images of something frail – a mustard seed – and something gigantic – a mountain. Faith, in Jesus' sense, moves mountains. It sees that there are no mountains or barriers between God and us. The mountains are imaginary.

Perhaps the theologians' problems arise because they search for a christology of Jesus as though it were separable from the christology of ordinary human beings. To be 'in Christ' can hardly mean to be in a permanent state of strain, feeling everlastingly inadequate in trying to follow another person who had an impossible advantage. It must mean, in some sense, the imparting of a state of consciousness 'which was in Christ Jesus.' Faith in Jesus would then involve a shattering and transformation of our sense of identity. As Watts puts the matter; ' "Christ" stands for the reality that there is no separate self to surrender. To give up "I" is a false problem. "Christ" is the realization that there is no separate "I." '[195] Jesus himself, from this standpoint, had an overwhelming experience of cosmic, centred consciousness, a sense of being totally at one with the universe. However, this event occurred in a culture which lacked a language and thought system to give it subtle expression without the use of great tact and the inevitable fate of being misunderstood. And misunderstood it was. The experience *of* Jesus – union with Godhood – became, in the Gospel, a message *about* him. Jesus becomes the believer's crutch rather than the spinal column. We might even say that the follower is to become

'Christ' rather than be a Christian.

If the theologian still wishes to talk about the incarnation we can see the sense of it, provided that it is understood to mean that the truth about existence is to be found in ourselves. Not the 'self,' of course, in the conventional sense. When the image of this self is shattered a new, deeper identity reveals itself. Watts puts it succinctly; 'God emptying himself to the limit is man, and man emptied to the limit is God.'[196] The great Carl Jung lamented the way in which Christ has so often been seen as an external reality. He says that

> too few people have experienced the divine image
> as the innermost possession of their own souls.
> Christ only meets them from without, never from
> within the soul![197]

Some readers may feel that the above paragraphs are just stating that Jesus is a 'mere' man as he appears to be in a great deal of contemporary theology. This would be an unfortunate impression. I have simply suggested that just as we need a changed sense of identity to understand the reality of God, so too we need something deeper than the conventional understanding of 'I' in order to see new depths in that reality we call 'Christ.' This consists in understanding 'Christ' as pointing to a transformed state of consciousness rather than to a particular historical person. The theologically conservative will suspect that I have reduced Jesus to the level of ordinary humanity. My aim, rather, has been to show that there is no such thing as 'ordinary humanity' except in the conventional sense. Jesus is not a 'mere' man since no person is a 'mere' person. Therefore, in a sense, it is humanity which is being raised rather than Jesus who is being reduced. On the other hand, I suspect that the theologically radical will accuse me of a modern brand of gnosticism. Any approach which smells faintly of the Orient or the mystical is bound to be cursed with this theological swear word at some time or other. The radicals will think that I have disembodied Jesus. For the life of me I cannot think why but I shall take up the charge of gnosticism later in the section discussing the problem of evil. I will simply comment here that, for all their apparent differences, the conservative and radical Christians accept the same basic understanding of the self. The conservatives often seem to turn the conventional self in on its own problems. The radicals turn the self outwards to face wider issues. Yet the self assumed by both groups is based on the model of severed consciousness. If we wished to be prickly the charge of gnosticism could be redirected back to the accusers who do not seriously wish to disturb society's disembodiment of our cosmic identity into the conventional I trapped in a bag of skin. I have tried to suggest that this is the self which Jesus bar Joseph said should not be improved but 'left behind.'

SALVATION – PARANOIA TO METANOIA

The doctrine of the incarnation, in traditional Christian thought, has addressed itself to a defect in the natural human condition. Humanity, it is said, needs to be redeemed or saved from the state of sin. The incarnation is a remedy for the human sickness. In John's gospel Jesus is told about the sickness of his friend Lazarus. On hearing the news, Jesus comments, 'This sickness is not unto death.' If physical illness is not the real sickness, what is? Jesus' reply has led people to wonder. Soren Kierkegaard said that it was despair and argued his case in his famous book *The Sickness Unto Death*. In the context of the present discussion, the malady could be regarded as a form of sleeping sickness for the living, missing life while life is there to be had. Man's bondage is not merely that he is imprisoned by his own selfish will – the fatal defect in Kierkegaard's phrase.

Where the religious analogies speak of the bondage of man they are about a conceptual rather than a moral captivity. We are spellbound by a false sense of identity. The hallucination is produced by consciousness identifying itself with one of its own ideas. The normal sense of 'I' is an abstraction based on memory. There can be no salvation through Christ, or any other being, unless we are redeemed from this conceptual death – the bondage to dead images. If our identity is not transformed out of that sense provided by social convention, no amount of effort to imitate Christ fundamentally changes anything. It may, indeed, produce a crippling sense of guilt. The hallucinatory 'I' is trying to imitate a selfless state which can only be if the 'I' does not exist. The ego is trying to be egoless.[198] This is paranoia, the mind beside itself, captivated by an image of itself. In biblical terms, metanoia is the mind with itself, no longer held captive by death and sin. Death is the realm of dead images and concepts, the realm of the remembered moment. When asked who they *are*, human beings are likely to reply with the description of who they *were*. They have identified with a dead image. We saw in the last section that, in Christian terms, the reality called 'Christ' is the end of the conceptual corpse called 'I.' As St. Paul put it; 'I live, yet no longer I; but Christ lives in me.'

Salvation then is the release from the mind's bewitched attachment to the unchanging image of what was. In one sense, it is anamnesis, a re-membering or recollection of the deep self that we were before we were dis-membered by the conventional self. It is a recollection of what the Buddhists might call the 'unborn mind.' Our true identity is unborn and unknown. We shall never be an object to ourselves. We cannot catch hold of ourselves and we have no need to. The sun does not need to shine on itself; it just shines. What we call normal life does not cease or become atomized if existence is understood in this way. We can see through the illusion and go back and enjoy it. We can play the game of 'I myself here and now' without, mercifully, the feeling that 'I' have to 'get something out of it,' as though the world were a bank to be robbed.

The reader may have listened patiently to all that has been said so far, but there is sure to be a question nagging in the background. Are we still dealing with merely human concerns which the author promised he would spare us? Is salvation, in other words, only for *this* world? One reply to this question could be that if we only hope in *this* world, we of all people are most to be pitied. *This* world is not *the* world. This world is the metred and measured conventional world of the normal state of consciousness. *The* world is the world as it *is*. It must be clear that we are not merely playing with words. When we experience the world as it is, we are living the life of heaven and eternity. I repeat, this is not just a way of speaking 'as if.' The crucial event is not the physical but the psychic death, the release from ego-enchantment.[199] What dies is just a set of thoughts of who we were. The traditional elements in the eschatological scheme are, therefore, to be understood in terms of changes in consciousness. The Last Day is the breakdown of our conventional sense of identity. The resurrection is the new birth of consciousness rather than the rebirth of the body. The life 'after death' is the 'now' in which there is no 'I.' A heaven after physical death suggests that there is something unfulfilled about the experience of the eternal now. Heaven is *beyond* the conventional future, but it is not *in* the future. Only Hell is in the future.[200] To live forever in the hope that heaven will arrive is to live in the hell of utter frustration. The ego lives on the circumference of the true self and frustrates itself with futile quests along that line. The kingdom of heaven is in the centre. Christianity invites us to 'ascend' with Christ to the centre of our deepest selves. There may be continuities after physical death but it is not an idea to which the liberated self will cling. As St. Paul put it; 'Now is the day of salvation.' The liberated cannot die. They are dead already, dead to the selves they are *said* to be.

The Spanish existentialist Miguel de Unamuno has an essay, 'Nicodemus the Pharisee' in which he says that 'in all of us there are two men, the temporal man and the eternal'[201]. Later in the same book he compares the temporal man to the dead Lazarus of John's gospel; 'Each man bears within him a Lazarus who needs only a Christ to resurrect him, and woe betide those poor Lazaruses who come to the end of their career of perceptible love and sorrow under the sun without ever having encountered a Christ to say to them: "Arise!" '[202] Salvation is a waking from sleep. Our sin is immortalized by the disciples in Gethsemane. Christ's question to them is the timeless question of the Christian religion; 'Could you not stay awake with me for one hour'?

WITNESSING CREATION

Consider this passage from the Zen Buddhist T'an-ching;

> In this moment there is nothing which comes to be. In this moment there is nothing which ceases to be. Thus there is no birth-and-death to be brought to an end. Wherefore the absolute tranquility is this present moment. Though it is at this moment, there is no limit to this moment, and herein is eternal delight.[203]

This is a crystal-clear expression of the sense of reality I have attempted to discuss throughout most of this study. Yet commonsense seems to say that of course there is something which comes to be. To have a present moment – however absolutely tranquil it be – implies that there was one 'before' it. Indeed, there must have been many successive moments before it. The world itself looks like an ancient remain that had its origin in the now far distant past.

Does it make sense to speak of creation from the point of view of transformed consciousness? In the latter state, we are told, all the realities about which religion speaks are present in the now moment. Do we have to make an exception on the subject of creation? It is quite possible to see how the incarnation, for example, could be understood as contemporaneous with our own being, but is not the creation a past event by definition? The mythological Adam and Eve were close to the origin but we are late on the scene. This is certainly the only acceptably sane view of most people in the

West, whether they talk about the origin in religious or purely natural terms. The world seems to have had a history and it is getting older and older.

I want to suggest a different way and one which sees the creation as contemporaneous with existence itself. It is necessary, first of all, to distinguish between what we could call the absolute and relative worlds. Genesis states that the world was 'without form and void.' It always is void and without form. In the absolute sense the world is simply there unnamed and undifferentiated. It does not have form; it is not even one or uniform. It simply *is*. It is void, empty of ways of seeing it. It is there to be seen. The relative world is the named and lesser creation, made up of things, events, facts. There is a creation within the absolute world which is 'no-thing.' The relative creation is produced by verbal, conventional distinctions 'by the Logos which is word-and-thought.'[204] This is the world we know with its boundaries and definitions. We *know* the absolute world too but in an obscure and neglected way. To know something in the ordinary sense is to be able to define it and we cannot know the absolute world in this way. Language is essentially dualistic. In this sense we all speak and think with forked tongues. It is only in the relative and dualistic sense that the world is old. From the absolute standpoint there is no then *and* now. The world is evoked by our senses in every moment. I may have the same paradisal view of the world as Adam in the garden. I may see the cycle of nature for what it is, a circle. The origin of a circle is any point on the circumference. From the mystical standpoint the world is always beginning now. Admittedly, like Adam after the fall, we normally live off centre, east of Eden in the relative world where the experience of the present is actually a memory of the immediate past.

We have, then, a two-eyed view of time. One eye is on the present and the other on the past or the future. To open the 'third eye' is to see beyond dualities. Our split sensation of time is symptomatic of a deeper, radical split. As D.T. Suzuki comments; 'All hope of Enlightenment is impossible while

Reality is divided into two opposites, subject and object, the thinker and the thought, the enquirer and his question.'[205] This idea, incidently, recalls the words of Jesus; 'If thine eye be single thy whole body will be full of light.' It is worthwhile considering too some remarks made by Ludwig Wittgenstein on the subject of creation. It is fairly clear that the idea of God's creating the world in some past time meant nothing to him. However, during a conversation with Friedrich Waismann, he made these remarks; 'For me the facts are unimportant. But what men mean when they say that "*The world is there*" lies close to my heart.'[206] In his lecture on ethics Wittgenstein discusses this feeling and says that it was, he believed, 'exactly what people were referring to when they said that God had created the world.'[207] The absolute world which is no-thing (sunyata) manifests itself as complete. It is simply there. There may be nothing new under the sun, but there is nothing old either.

THE BIG WORRY

In my own experience, whenever people discuss the kind of view with which this book deals there is one issue which often dominates all others. This is the question of suffering and evil. This is the great nagging worry. Failure to give an adequate explanation for suffering and evil would be *the* flaw in the system. Thinkers like Alan Watts and Krishnamurti – indeed all mystics – are invariably suspected of being curiously insensitive to the painful realities of the world. Take, for example, Kenneth Leech's comments in *The Social God*. The latter is a discussion of the incarnation in the light of a proposed new synthesis of the mystical and the political. Leech finds in Watts' writings 'a frightening disregard for human suffering, for the poor, the oppressed, the small man.'[208] The theological swear term used to damn Watts' position is 'Gnostic anti-materialism.' When seen through the eyes of this philosophy 'the poor man is dispensable.' By contrast, the life of incarnation is, apparently, involved, prophetic and caring. This, I suggest, is a disastrous misunderstanding of Watts in particular and the realization approach in general. It is, as I have said, a very common reaction to any standpoint which looks vaguely oriental. Enlightenment, realization, liberation – whatever the description happens to be – is really, it is said, just a high-brow way of learning not to care. It is not concerned with true liberation from the real bondage of social injustice and all the other forms of human misery. It seeks a purely inward, self-indulgent illumination, a mere shampoo and manicure for the mystic's own soul. So the argument goes. Nevertheless, if the view I have expounded is to be damned, it should at least be damned for what it claims to be. It should not, emphatically not, be classified as an exotic brand of 'personal inward religion' found among the more depressing brands of Evangelical Protestant Christianity. The latter *are* often politically naive and blind to the social structures which do ensure that the poor receive more than their share of injustice and pain. This has been demonstrated countless times, the more obvious ones being its impotency in the face of Hitler's fascism and in the midst of racialist systems throughout the modern world. Leech, like many others before him, does not appear to have understood the radicality of the so called way of realization. It is not another form of 'inward' pietistic renewal. It is a complete re-casting of the commonsense state of consciousness which removes the idea that evil and suffering are ultimately tragic. Watts and company want to say that fundamentally all *is* well. It is not that all *shall* be well as some Christian theodicies have attempted to show. It is that all is well *now*. Leech, and many others, presumably want to know how a sensitive person could mean that in view of the presence of evil and suffering in the world. Kenneth Leech, for example, claims that suffering is an illusion on Watts' view. But this is to misunderstand. Pain and suffering are real. What is illusory is our way of classifying it. The world is real but the description of it is illusion or *maya*. It makes perfect sense to distinguish

between good and evil, pain and pleasure but these are relative and not absolute distinctions. They are classifications
within what we could call the dual realm in which experience
is conditioned by its opposite – pleasure and pain, life and
death, youth and age, joy and sorrow, good and evil. From
the point of view of the way of realization, anyone who
makes his or her happiness dependant upon one of these
opposites is doomed to frustration. To be the play of limited
states of salvation is to be subject to the ups and downs of
samsara. The experience of realization, of non-duality, sees
beyond classifications and, therefore, beyond good and evil.
To call one act good and another evil is to isolate aspects of
one total happening which in reality has no separable aspects.
This is not to say that evil acts are morally acceptable but to
say that none of them can fundamentally disrupt the complete
unity of the whole.

Christian theologians have made much of the distinction
between good and evil. The first of these two opposites is
desirable and the difference looks impressive. The problem of
evil and suffering is commonly regarded as the great problem
facing the theologian defending what I have called the God of
severed consciousness. How could such a God tolerate both
uncontrolled deliberate malice and unrelieved purposeless
suffering? The theologian, it seems, cannot do with evil and
yet cannot do without it. There is a story which illustrates the
schizophrenic attitude of Christianity towards evil. A priest is
late for service. As he runs towards the church he sees a
severely wounded man, close to death. Momentarily he is
torn between his duty to lead worship and that of helping the
dying man. He decides on the latter but backs away as he
recognizes the man to be the devil. The priest runs towards
the church but the devil calls after him; 'Listen priest! If I die,
if evil dies, where will your God be? If evil dies, how will you
know what is good? You exist because of me. Think about it.'
The priest admits the logic and returns to save the devil and
his own religion.

Christianity maintains an absolute duality. Good and evil,

it seems, represent a split in reality itself. The ways of realization appear to imply that if reality is fundamentally non-dual there can be no such split. Consequently, they do not seem to take evil seriously. There would be no objection presumably if we lived in a paradisal situation of total harmony. 'All shall be well' in paradise, perhaps. But not here. R.C. Zaehner has argued that Zen, for example, is precisely just such a philosophy for people 'before the fall.' The theologian Harvey Cox, in his study of oriental philosophies, tends to agree with this;

> Zen resolutely holds to a vision which deals with pain, desire, choice, loss and tragedy in such a way that, while it does not deny their reality, it does not affirm it either.... It is a spirituality for saints and innocents, and insofar as all of us sinners maintain at least a memory or an intuition of that innocence, Zen will always have an appeal. The trouble is that most of us live 'after the fall,' and, if that is true, a mode of existence based on innocence can become both a temptation and a torture. Most of us need a religion for sinners....
> To say we live in a 'fallen world' means that we find ourselves in a cosmos where that primal unity that Zen allows us to glimpse is broken. It is broken, furthermore, not just because something is askew in our perception of it, but because something is askew in the thing itself.[209]

This is a clear statement of the issue I have attempted to discuss. On the traditional Christian view the division between good and evil, between unalloyed bliss and meaningless suffering reflects a fracture in reality itself. It is not something a good God could tolerate for the sake of a wider harmony. As Dostoyevsky's character would say, it would not justify one child's tear.

Throughout this study I have attempted to discuss a state of consciousness which is non-conceptual, an experience of the absolute and non-dual nature of reality. To the unenlightened mind the normal world is a world of opposites where the differences are real and appear absolute. The enlightened person lives simultaneously in the absolute and relative worlds. Where there is suffering he or she does everything possible to alleviate it. There is no reason why anyone who experiences the absolute, centred state of consciousness should be paralyzed in the face of suffering and evil. For Christianity the issue between the children of light and the children of darkness is a desperately serious one. From the point of view of the realized state, it is belief in separate realities which is at the heart of the problem. Earlier in this chapter I discussed the questions of christology and had cause to notice that, despite their differences, both conservative and radical Christians were fundamentally united in their understanding of the self. A similar thing has to be said about the children of light and darkness. In the voices and prose of the radical and revolutionary children of the light it is possible to hear the click of the jackboot and the rattle of rifle bolts. Under different social conditions they could easily be arguing for the position they now despise. It is said that American Indians, when trying to discover whether a stranger was a friend or an enemy, used to ignore his words and listen to his tone of voice. If we adopt the same way of listening to two groups bitterly divided over a major issue we can, I suggest, see similarities between them which reveals a deep underlying agreement about the nature of the self. Turn down the sound of a televised debate and look at the gestures and facial expressions of the people involved. Why should it be so difficult to decide which person is arguing which case? It is possible to oppose a particular form of human oppression and, at the same time, be an unconscious conspirator in an understanding of the self which is fundamentally anti-human and which may be at the source of much of the hell being raised on this planet. This may be why Krishnamurti sometimes says that some people rob banks while others become social workers, implying that there is a connection between the two.

The children of light hope to defeat the children of darkness. Their behaviour is different but their state of consciousness may be basically the same. It seems possible, on both views, to shatter the unity of the world in a quite fundamental sense. This is only so, however, if our conceptual distinctions actually correspond to divisions in reality. Where this is the case, the world does, indeed, look like a chocolate orange which, if hit in the appropriate place, will fall into segments. Fractured lives reflect the fracture at the tragic heart of reality itself. The enlightened or realized person denies this. On his view no victim's life has been a tragedy in the absolute sense, although it may be said to have been in a relative sense. He or she has eternal dignity no matter what their fate. It is said, for example, that many Jews laughed at their murderers as they were being butchered in Nazi Germany. This is the laugh of the absolute. It is a refusal to accept their captors' definition of reality. It is to deny that the reality experts are those with the big clubs. How dare anyone deny such victims the right to say that all is well in my life despite the diabolical crimes you are about to commit against me? They deserve, at least, to be able to say that. To succumb to the feeling that any victim's life has been a tragedy in an absolute sense is to acquiesce to a death deeper than the physical one. As far as I can see, the writings of Alan Watts and Krishnamurti support just such a denial of total, unrelieved tragedy. Anyone is entitled to discover in the midst of their winter – to use Camus' words – an unconquerable summer. Why this should be thought of as treating suffering as illusion is beyond me. The point I have been trying to make in the last few paragraphs could be made less dramatically by referring to the dying words of Ludwig Wittgenstein. He was dying of cancer and just before he lost consciousness he said, 'Tell them I've had a wonderful life!'[210] These words were meant for his friends. One of them, Norman Malcolm, writes, 'When I think of his profound pessimism, the intensity of his mental and moral suffering, the relentless way in which he drove his intellect, his need for love together with the harshness that repelled love, I am inclined to believe that his life was fiercely unhappy.'[211] Yet

Wittgenstein himself said that it had been 'wonderful.' Should Malcolm have said, 'No, it hasn't'? Malcolm's actual response to Wittgenstein's words was, 'To me this seems a mysterious and strangely moving utterance.'[212] Wittgenstein was using the language of the absolute.

Let me attempt to summarize. The smile on the face of the Buddha means that he is serene, not that he doesn't care. To sense an identity with all living things means, at the same time, to feel compassion. If I commit a mean, cruel act it means the deep sense of identity is not there or has lapsed. If we understand ourselves as fundamentally an expression of the ground of the universe, we all share the universal suffering of every living thing. In this sense there is no single victim. Nevertheless, no one can deny that basic to many of the conventional games we play is the move 'victim.' Since most of us play this game, we pay the price of having a conventional sense of identity which gives this move its meaning. Part of the price, of course, is the agony of witnessing the suffering of the victim. The feeling of being healthy must include the possibility of being in agony. To suffer is to be acutely conscious, whether this is dying of stomach cancer or being crucified under Pontius Pilate. It *forces* us to give up the ghost of the conventional self. We cannot hold on. Whether the healthy like it or not, people who know they are terminally ill often behave in a very liberated way, looking bemused at the falling rocks clutched by the terminally well.

At the heart of all human problems, and that of suffering is no exception, there stands the question, 'Who are you?' Just where are we to draw up the focus and say, 'That's me there, I hurt and I have problems, not least those of suffering and dying.' But this begs the question; why draw the focus so myopically? Conflict at one level is harmony at another. Which level of magnification is right? There are, for example, continuous battles in the bloodstream. If I take a microscopic view of 'myself' I shall probably identify with one set of corpuscles and forget how healthy I am at a much higher level. Conflicts at whatever level may be capped by broader harmonies up to the Supreme Self of the so called way of realization. As hard as this may sound to the ego, the 'cramp in consciousness' to use Jung's phrase, what is tragedy at one level is ecstasy at another. Death is usually regarded as an undesirable, if inevitable, event. But it is possible to imagine, in theory at least, a unanimity about breaking up or death as a good thing – the ecstasy of disappearing. As I say, this is too much for the self of ordinary awareness. It is always difficult to accept death in the young or seemingly meaningless suffering and agony. We would have to experience the intermediate stage first, of seeing the world just as it is, in its thusness or suchness as the Buddhists say.

ON LOVING AND NEVER FORGIVING

Despite everything that has been said so far, many readers may wish to press the question, 'How is all of this supposed to affect our lives?' Is it, in other words fruitful in producing desirable changes at the personal and social levels? In some ways, to ask this question at all is to have missed the point of all the previous chapters. It is not a doctrine which can be *applied to* the world. To think in such terms is still to be a victim of the illusory notion that you are separate from a world which is to be affected or changed in some way. In one sense, the only answer to the question is that which Alan Watts himself gave sometimes; 'Be there, and see what happens.' This, however, is not much help for the person who is still asking the question.

One blunt answer to the question is that the sensation of a deep identity is a truer basis for love and concern than the fiction of the separate ego. To use dual and relative terms; the realization of the supreme identity offers the only real possibility of an ultimately sane and peaceful state of affairs on this planet. True love comes from identity and knowledge, not from duty or the guilty feeling that I must love. Krishnamurti would probably call this the 'only revolution' – a revolution in consciousness. It is the mystical rather than the practical view which is truly revolutionary. The mystical approach sees the world as it *is* – free from the 'known' thoughts, the thieves of consciousness. One can easily imagine someone seeing the point of these remarks and saying, 'Fine, that's true, but how exactly can I be a subversive contemplative?' as though it were something one could decide to become. Mysticism is not yet another ideology or scalpel with which to go to work on the world's ills. Rather it is a perspective from within which we may see just how destructive righteous ideas can be. It would be a depressing task to catalogue all the well-intentioned ideologies, Christian or otherwise, which have been pursued in the name of progress and goodwill. Revolutions have the habit of running backwards and down. As R.H.Blyth writes; 'Forgive us our good deeds, as we forgive those we do good deeds to us.'[213] The mystical view need not paralyze us but it may make our ways of interfering more intelligent.

At the heart of the mystical view is the understanding that life is essentially mysterious. As Wittgenstein said, *that* the world is rather than *how*, is the mystical. Together with this there is the sense that time is somehow an illusion. We are never given three moments; the past, present and the future. We always have only one moment, now. In this light, fellow humans have a mysterious, timeless quality. When the sense of mystery leaves us we may become bored with them. We may, too, resent some of their actions. Krishnamurti said that where there is love there is no forgiveness. Someone who truly lives in the present, choicelessly aware, does not store up an account of wrongs which may or may not evoke his or her forgiveness. Without a change in consciousness, even the most dutiful following of a moral code is a way of putting life on 'automatic' and of being dead in terms of the present moment. As Alan Watts comments; 'Nothing is really more inhuman than human relations based on morals. When a man gives bread in order to be charitable, lives with a woman in order to be faithful, eats with a Negro in order to be unprejudiced. . .he is as cold as a clam. He does not actually see the other person.'[214] We are talking about an uncalculated life in the present in which the act is simultaneous with the intention. A great deal of popular Christian moral teaching seems curiously blind to this, concerned as it is with the transformation of behaviour rather than that of consciousness. Purity of heart involves both forms of transformation. The world has suffered enough from good people in the singular sense.

When reading through books on Christian ethics for doctrines of forgiveness it is interesting to ask whether the belief in eternal damnation is held to. It is, in fact, often strangely present despite the wholesale reinterpretation or rejection of many other traditional doctrines. It is not, of course, spoken of in the same way that preachers used to describe the dungeons of heaven. The language is much more subtle. As a student, I vividly remember something called the 'Paul Tillich Game.' Tillich was famous for reinterpreting the Christian doctrine of grace in terms of acceptance; simply accept the fact that you are accepted. The game consisted in imagining God to say 'You are accepted' as he shook the hands of the dead as they walked through the pearly gateway. The question was whether you could imagine God declining to shake hands with someone. Regular candidates were super-sinners like Hitler and Stalin. Since then I have heard people unintentionally playing the same game. I once listened to a rabbi deliver a lecture on the Jewish understanding of the world to come. During the questions which followed, a member of the audience was astonished to hear the rabbi say that Hitler would make it eventually. When asked why, the rabbi explained that Jews believe in tolerance and equality. I tried the same question myself after listening to successive talks by another rabbi and a radical Christian. This time, however, both speakers agreed that Hitler stood no chance. It is possible, it seems, for individuals to fracture reality and slip through the crack. I mention this here simply to draw attention to the differing views of two men, both rabbis, who were well aware of the atrocities carried out by Hitler, yet who came to different conclusions about his ultimate fate. The first rabbi seemed to offer more hope despite his awareness of what his people had suffered under Nazism. This brings us back to the problem of evil again but there is no space here to continue with this particular issue.

It is impossible to discuss human relations in the context of the way of realization without putting them against the background of our total ecology – the so-called natural world. We have seen how people are often subjected to ideas we have *about* them. The natural world suffers a similar fate. A simple example will make the point. There was once an art competition in New York and each student was given a cubic foot of plaster of Paris. The winner, a girl, looked at the cube and asked herself, 'What does this cube want to be?' At that moment, it appeared to her, it did not want to be anything. She dropped it on the floor. After looking at the partly shattered cube she said, 'I see what it wants to be now.' We could say, similarly, that the most compassionate attitude towards the natural world is to ask what it wants to be. Views which are dominated by the illusion of the separate ego tend to adapt the environment to fit human aspirations oblivious to our place in the symbiosis of patterns and the natural harmony of the universe. There are two short anecdotes which illustrate the two contrasting approaches to nature in vivid ways. The first is about unintelligent interference and a general mistrust of the natural world. A farmer's son arrived late for tea and his father wondered why. The son explained that he had been helping the corn to grow. The farmer looked a little puzzled but carried on with his meal. The following morning he found that all the wheat was dead. 'I thought you said that you were helping the corn to grow?' The son replied, 'I was. Last night I went round each small wheat shoot and pulled it up slightly.' The second story is about making decisions more in accord with the flow of nature. The subjects of an Indian king complained that the rough ground was cutting and hurting their bare feet. In an effort to relieve their pains, the king proposed to spread many thousands of animal skins all over the surface of the land. His adviser, however, had a better idea. Why not use a few animal skins to cut out shapes to tie under people's feet – sandals!

Both stories are, of course, Taoist in spirit. The Taoist approach, with it awareness of natural rhythms, contrasts very strongly with the western tendency to treat the world as a clock-work orange, an object subject to the whims of humanity. It may be that space exploration has accentuated this tendency. The earth looks more like an object than ever. Some Christian theologians have been sensitive to these possibilities. Paul Tillich makes the point;

> One of the results of the flight into space and the possibility of looking down at the earth is a kind of estrangement between man and earth, an 'objectification' of the earth for man, the depriving 'her' of her 'motherly' character, her power of giving birth, of nourishing, of embracing, of keeping for herself, of calling back to herself. She becomes a large, material body to be looked at and considered as totally calculable.[215]

What if the earth is indeed seen as a body, a mother? What sort of organism would the human race be? Would it be good or harmful bacteria? In one sense there can never be anything unnatural in the world. To use one of Alan Watts' metaphors; as an apple tree *apples*, so the universe *peoples*. Yet some things that people do are less natural than others. To use an untypically mystical term for the moment, the 'ideal' person is the Taoist cloud-water man. He drifts like a cloud and flows like water. This image is more in accord with the natural flow of the universe than that which holds up the ideal of our deliberately embracing holy poverty;

> Somehow one feels in the Christian emphasis on poverty that poverty contrasts with richness as good to evil. In other words, poverty is unpleasant but it is something you ought to share with

the poor who live unpleasant lives, so if you are to
expiate your sins you ought to be poor and to live
roughly. And for this reason in Buddhism one
would not say poverty, but rather simplicity. Not
going without, not avoiding clinging to things
because its good to do so, but because it is actually
the happiest way to live, because nothing is more
terrifying than the state of chronic anxiety which
one has if you are subject to the illusion that something or other in life could be held on to and safe-
guarded. . .and nothing can. So the acceptance of
everything flowing away is absolutely basic to
freedom.[216]

The Zen master Shuuryu Suzuki said, 'Renunciation is not
giving up the things of this world, it is accepting that they go
away.' Barry Stevens makes the same point throughout her
book, *Don't Push the River*, in which she uses the insights of
Zen, Krishnamurti and the American Indian to show the
possibility of a reversal in our western self-understanding and
our good intentions for this planet;

We clutter our lives and neurotically moan or
groan about our burdens. Like the white man's
burden to louse up the world instead of letting it
be. Now we're cluttering up the stratosphere and
the moon. Don't give me that stuff about 'You can't
stop progress.' All we have to do is stop calling it
progress.[217]

All such talk about letting things be will sound like callous
passivity to some ears. But she is really making the point that
our troubles lie rooted in the way we understand ourselves
and the natural world. She discusses the American Indian's
understanding of the latter and comments; ' "Indian" is not
skin color. It is a way of living which does not lead to
Vietnam.'[218]

Is there any conclusion to be drawn from this very brief discussion of Christian ethics? What can be said here is closely linked to the discussion of Christ at the beginning of the chapter. Demands to imitate the deeds of Jesus are not radical enough. They resemble the act of painting the shadow in order to improve the person. The fiction of the separate ego in a bag of skin is just such a shadow. Christ-like deeds flow naturally from a Christ-like state of consciousness. The action is simultaneous with the intention. To deny this possibility to any person seems, to me at least, like denying the central and radical truth of Christianity. The living water which makes their deeds truly lively and truly theirs is being denied. They are destined to be permanently parched, despite the promise that they would never thirst again. It is hardly surprising that so many today look to quench their thirst through the help of aquarian water bearers outside the Christian tradition.

SUNDAY MORNING

So far in this chapter I have made a few brief comments about some of the traditional aspects of the Christian analogy as they might appear in the light of the views discussed throughout this book. If Christians did look at their faith in this way would it affect what they did on Sunday mornings? What, in other words, would be the implications for Christian spirituality, for the life of worship and devotion? This is a subject for study in its own right, involving the whole tradition of contemplative spirituality. In any case, I am hardly qualified to say. I shall simply make a few observations for what they are worth. It could be added too that the question is very hypothetical and unrealistic. Surveying the present ecclesiastical scene, the possibilities of an outbreak of contemplative mysticism seem rather remote.

There are some obvious questions to ask. Would one of the implications of the view I have examined be a wholesale reform of the liturgy? Another would be about the place of prayer. Does it still make sense to pray? Indeed, does the whole notion of worship itself make sense? There can be no general answer to these questions. For some, the experience of expanded consciousness could make private prayer super-fluous. They may feel that it introduces a needless dualism. This appears to have been the case for Alan Watts. In his autobiography he comments that while he could take part with delight in the formal liturgy of public worship;

> the Christian style of the interior life went com-pletely against the grain...personal talking and praying to God in so many words just isn't in my nature. I feel it as a clumsy encumbrance which not only puts God at a distance but also treats him as another person or creature, however exalted and holy, and distracts one from the realization that 'God is nearer to you than you are to your-self.' Personal prayer simply got in the way of my fundamental mystical feeling that God is what there is and all that there is.[219]

This would not be everyone's experience. Alan Watts was deeply influenced by the Buddhist traditions and this is very evident in the above passage. If one does feel oneself to be fundamentally at one with the divine ground of the universe it may seem 'a pity to say so' – to oneself. Others may, of course, take great delight in saying so. The point is that the private or public expression of devotion or worship should be natural and not forced. In another book Watts comments on the liturgical reforms which attempt to enable the congrega-tion to participate in rather merely observe a sacerdotal drama;

> The Church cannot celebrate a truly radial Mass without a shift in spiritual experience parallel to the shift in ritual. It is an empty gesture to move the altar to the center of the church without that changed sense of identity in which God is found to

be the center of man. Otherwise, the altar at the center is still being treated as the altar at the East, where God is approached as an external and imperious power, an alien authority who judges and compels us from beyond and above.[220]

Worship then may be as natural as any activity of human beings. It is an expression of gratitude for the existence of the world. It is a celebration for its own sake. Many people, of course, may not see it in this way. Such a way of speaking would be appropriate if we were standing in the middle of the beatific vision. But we are not, they may say. Nevertheless, let me refer back to a distinction I drew earlier, in chapter five, when discussing the nature of religious language. If the supreme reality of which religion speaks is felt to be not quite present or unrealized, then religious language will be *referential*. The words will be thought to point to a reality not immediately experienced. However, in certain states of consciousness the status of the language is changed. It is *itself expressive* of the experience of realization. The religious doctrines and statements are then *analogies* of a state of realization deeper than the descriptions of it. We could apply the distinction to worship in a similar way. If the religious reality is not totally present then the act of worship will be *about* that reality. Indeed, believers often speak of worship as a 'recharge for the spiritual batteries.' This way of speaking turns the act of worship into a cultural act of defiance. A spiritually refreshed person is preparing to struggle with a world which is fundamentally non-religious. But what if a believer sees the so-called everyday world as, in fact, the beatific vision? Worship will then be a celebration of the vision. It will *in itself* be expressive in *sacramental* terms of the reality which is expressed *analogically* through religious language. So understood, religion is not *about* existence. It is a form of existence. It does not mean something; it *confers* meaning.

Any discussion of spirituality and worship is bound to raise questions about the place and role of the clergy in all of this. This, again, is a far ranging issue and I will be content with a few remarks. This study has been critical at several points of the way in which the theologians have succumbed to standard non-religious definitions of reality. Have the parsons faired any better? From the perspective of this present study, we are bound to say that their capitulation has been institutional and therefore more visible than the theologians.' To be fair, it has to be said that many parsons agonize over their own role. The sense of guilt and impotence runs very deep in that profession. What self-confidence there is among them derives, I would say, largely from their ability to compete with or complement the role of the social worker. Few people, I suspect, expect a parson to say something which would seriously undermine the normal state of consciousness. By and large they plead for changes in behaviour and repeat, with less confidence, things which are worthy of belief. In my own experience theology is not a burning topic in clerical circles. By theology I do not mean the contents of the latest theological book, but the deep resources of the faith once delivered to the saints which profoundly challenge the conventional state of mind. There is plenty of advice for tactics and attitudes towards international issues, personal and social problems but very little available for those who want to see through these particular games and ask 'Who am I *really*?' or, indeed, 'Who or what is God?' During a televised interview the novelist John Updike was asked why his books contained so many parsons and why they appeared in such a bad light. His reply would sound cruel to any parson who happened to be watching but it casts some light on the issue here. Updike said that most clergymen he had met were not particularly deep human beings and that he was fascinated by people in bonds. Parsons were, he said, men in very visible social bonds. This is a very ironical charge but one which comes close to the mark. It applies not just to the predictability of the day to day ecclesiatical tasks and the parson's role but also to what he stands for. Even the most radical members of the full time ministry are depressingly amenable to the conventional sociological and psychological definitions of the self.

I think it is worth making one final comment. From the perspective of the mystical view the issues I have mentioned in this section are not problems at all in a real sense. The questions of church unity, order and the role of the parson are not that important and certainly hardly worth a lifetime's worry. If we wish to see the church and the Christian religion in problematic terms the real issue is whether it has anything of fundamental rather than of conventional importance to say about the nature of existence. We can see the issue in more concrete terms by glancing through the early sections of Carl Jung's reminiscences of his childhood included in *Memories, Dreams, Reflections*. Jung saw the conventional side of Christianity in close-up. Several members of his mother's family were parsons as indeed was his own father. Jung speaks of the stale and hollow version of religion preached by his father, who was, Jung concedes, a good man; 'He did a great deal of good – far too much – and as a result was usually irritable.'[221] Jung's criticisms of conventional Christianity resemble D.H. Lawrence's reaction to the tiresome platitudes of the preachers in the Nottingham chapels. Jung had glimpsed a secret, a lost Christianity which his clerical relations were sublimely unaware of. He listened to their sermons and theological conversations and observes that 'whenever I listened to them I had the feeling: "Yes, yes, that is all very well. But what about the secret?.... None of you know anything about that." '[222] Jung read books by theologians in his father's library but always found himself thinking, 'They don't know either.' Jung's criticisms, I believe, amount to the charge that Christianity too readily conforms to what is thought to be discoverable. It needs to be free from the known and the temptation to provide merely a slightly more profound version of the expected. Its attempts to provide the *truth* often sound like ways of matching the thoughts we already have. Why, we may ask, does St. John have Jesus silent before Pilate's question? What if Jesus *had* replied? The words would have belonged to Jesus but the meanings of those words would have been provided by Pilate. Seen in this way, this encounter is a deeply symbolic event. Perhaps Pilate should have asked Jung's question before leaving the room. What about the secret? A person asking this question is open to surprise.

7 World making and the secular swamis

THE PREVIOUS CHAPTER may have meant little to many readers. The modern world, we are told, is not religious. This has been assumed as a self evident fact by countless individuals since the late nineteenth century. Intellectuals have repeated the message ad nauseam through the language of their own specialisms. The world may be taken to be material, ordinary, self-explanatory unless shown to be otherwise. If religion has something to say it must make out a case against an everyday sense of reality, often felt as threatening, but which is safe, certain and unproblematic in its own way. The religious person, it is said, lives with what is *as if* whereas the non-religious person lives with what *is*. The philosophical, psychological and sociological critiques of religion have largely agreed in their assessment of the nature and function of religion. The 'as if' statements of religion are, in reality, only fanciful ways of talking about 'what is.' In other words, the so-called religious realities can be reduced to a more substantial, non-religious baseline. The religious notion of remorse, for example, would be classified as unproductive guilt. Sin would be misdemeanour explicable within the context of a complicated network of personal and social circumstances. The movement towards the baseline is relentless. I once had a depressing conversation with a child psychologist on the apparently barely numinous subject of charm. 'Ah,' he commented at one point, 'What you call charm I call social skill.' There was nothing I could say which would dissuade him from thinking that the former was only an extravagant way of speaking about the latter. I felt helpless too when a mathematics student insisted that the universe was really just a machine.

To argue against such reductionist views of the universe could make one feel like a witch doctor confronting a nuclear scientist. This shows just how strong the commonsense approach to reality has become. I hope that the previous chapters have shown how metaphysical and mythological such an approach is in reality. There is no assumption about the world which is not philosophical. To say that the world is material or physical is to have philosophical ideas *about* the world. To insist that the world *is* material is to confuse the description with the reality; to confuse conceiving with perceiving. There is no neutral, ordinary, philosophically innocent experience of the world which is safe and sure over against the speculations of religion. To shun philosophical discussion altogether with 'I'm basically just a practical person' is merely to be disinterested in examining the deeply rooted philosophical assumptions which underly such a remark. To insist on non-religious, philosophically neutral territory is, I believe, to succumb to the 'craving for generality' which Wittgenstein spoke about. His philosophy was used in chapter three to resist the longing for an all embracing concept of reality in the light of which a whole range of claims to reality could be judged. It is simply not possible to put all world pictures side by side in a wider framework and so judge them by a context-free, absolute standard. The latter would merely be another world picture. Some have seen this way of looking at the issue as a sympathetic and promising perspective on the moral and religious spheres in particular. It preserves their sui generis character. More often, however, it produces a sinking feeling in those who want to hold on to truth in these spheres. Do we have just a variety of pictures or views *of* the world? Can we be said to have a world at all? Is my view ultimately and simply my view? Nelson Goodman, in his book *Ways of World Making* considers these questions and comments that 'the philosopher like the philanderer is always finding himself stuck with none or too many.'[223]

It is, of course, the sociologists who have rubbed in the message in concrete ways not normally accessible to the philosopher. Reality, we are told, is socially constructed. A person's sense of reality depends upon the group which provides a 'plausibility structure.' The sociology of knowledge reveals a plurality of life-worlds. It has spelt out in plain language what many have felt in their bones. Religion does not give ultimate certainty in face of the exigences of the total human condition. It merely makes one experience of reality *plausible* to one group; 'Any kind of consciousness is plausible only in particular social circumstances.'[224] This quotation is from a study of the sociological analysis of consciousness and reveals just how broadly some sociologists view their field of investigation. There is, however, a very obvious question to ask. In what state of consciousness does the sociologist study other people's states of consciousness? We need to heed the words of Alan Watts mentioned earlier. He warns us to beware of the next passing swami who, while trying to show us what is going on behind the social facade of self-identity, actually sells us still another institutionalized version of the real world. The sociologist is a strong candidate for the role of swami. To use the terms of two widely read sociologists, definitions of reality are imposed by those with the bigger sticks.[225] The sociologists have rather large sticks themselves. The more sensitive among them wield their sticks with 'cognitive nervousness,'[226] but, by and large, their descriptions of the plurality of world views offer, by implication, a more plausible picture than any particular world view could present. The world is simply a place which contains views of what reality is supposed to be. To know this is, again by implication, to know more than those in the grip of any particular plausibility structure. This is the swami speaking. It is a conventional view of the world. D.Z. Phillips has argued forcefully to show how the sociologist offers us a persuasive, charming and dangerous story by impoverishing the mode of discourse it claims to analyse. He calls it the 'sociologizing of meaning' and claims that it 'blinds us to other possibilities of meaning, and is both the agent and the product of the very alienation from which it claims to offer liberation.'[227] It has unspoken, subterranean assumptions about the world.

The sociologist's story has proved seductive. It has sapped the confidence more dramatically than all the speculations of Kant. Woody Allen put the matter colourfully;

> Can we actually 'know' the universe? My God, it's hard enough finding your way around in China-town. The point, however, is: Is there anything out there? And why? And must they be so noisy?[228]

THE CURE FOR EDUCATION

If the above paragraphs carry any weight they show how even the most secular education – whether formally in institutions or informally in families – looks like an initiation into a religion. Take, for example, the most practical, down to earth course for preparing children for their future adult lives. The anticipated conditions may not, in fact, materialize but the child's consciousness will be subtly influenced in his or her experience of the present. Years of gazing at forthcoming attractions may make them incapable of appreciating the main feature when it supposedly 'arrives.' A state of consciousness is nurtured in the child which he or she rarely has cause to question throughout adult life. In this century we have learned just how complicated child development can be. As someone shrewdly observed; 'Understanding the secrets of the atom is child's play compared with understanding child's play.' One thing is clear, at least. As children we had no antidote to words. On being told what something is, babies are never heard to say 'I doubt it.' We are not, of course, simply being given conventional labels such as 'chair' and 'spoon.' We are being sold a much more profound convention, namely, how objects, events and actions are to be delineated and given a range of meaning in our experience of the world. The construction of the conceptual scaffolding is sustained over many years becoming increasingly labyrinthine. The scaffolding itself becomes an occupied building, an edifice which hides the original. Thoughts cast a veil over the real.

A different image will possibly make the point more vividly to someone unfamiliar with the issue here. Imagine a photograph of a person or an object. Under high magnification the picture is seen to be made up of dots. It would be foolish to think that the person or the object were composed of dots too. Think of the world as the 'unspeakable' reality to be 'pictured' by our conceptual descriptions whose 'dots' are the notions of thing, fact, event and so on. Is it not as mistaken to think that reality is somehow made up of things, for example, as to think that the person or object is made up of dots? Words and concepts do have a reality of their own kind. They too are in the world. Yet the reality to which they point is not itself an idea.

The things that were said to us as children were irresistible. After all, we had nothing with which to resist them. By the time we have acquired a language it is too late. We bought the language at the price of accepting its tacit assumptions about the world. How then can we challenge the grip of these assumptions in the terms of the language? It is as though a solid image could be confronted by its own shadow. To change the metaphor, would it not be like a character in a dream instructing the dreamer to wake up, breaking the spell in the language of the incantation which spellbinds? Kierkegaard once asked how it is possible to wake up someone who is dreaming that they are awake.

What we find irresistible is not simply a way of talking. It is a way of being, a state of consciousness. Its freedom is that which a child has when presented with a picture colouring book. He or she has a choice of colours, even of shading, but the boundaries are clearly marked out in black borders. In a similar way, the conceptual apparatus we adopt outlines the manner in which the world is classified and to be experienced. We paint by numbers and experience the world on the tram-lines of thought. It is true that people often say that they have changed their minds. It would be more appropriate to say that they have changed their ideas. The state of mind or consciousness is basically undisturbed. The change is merely a different dream in the same dream-like state. The state of mind in which the description is confused with the real has, in fact, often been compared to sleep. Dreams keep us sleepy during the night; thoughts keep us sleepy during the day. Timothy Leary has called it the 'ontological sleep' and, as is widely known, had some very controversial ways of rousing the sleeper.[229]

Leary's experiments were not surprisingly subversive to the educational establishment. However, quite apart from drastic methods of awakening, the very idea that what is innocently called ordinary, everyday experience should be a state of sleep is subversive. It involves a shift in consciousness in which thought itself undergoes a change in status. To some-one who identifies his or her thoughts about the world with the world itself, such a change could seem like the *end* of the world and, therefore, not a serious possibility. Imagine babies being reared in a huge glass incubator which they never leave. Imagine too that they are educated inside it. Their teacher introduces them to the outside world by painting images on the glass which exactly correspond with the outside world as it appears to someone inside. The teacher may conceivably have a machine which projects images in natural colours on to the glass and which always follow whatever movements there are outside. When the process is complete there is a perfect copy of the 'real' world on the glass. Their education is complete. But, to their astonishment, the teacher tells them that they are now ready for the second stage in their educa-tion, namely, scraping the glass clean of paint or living with-out the moving projections. It would seem like a threat to end their world. But since the images on the glass are experienced as the world *itself*, the teacher appears to be talking nonsense. One can imagine the teacher's pleas. Wouldn't they rather see the real world than a picture of it? The children, however, would have no means of understanding this distinction. It would not be a rational choice granted their present state of consciousness. In one sense their education would have made them 'life proof.'

Almost everyone reading this book will agree that no such radical change of consciousness is proposed by the tutor or looked for by the taught in the usual course of education. New and surprising things are learned within a framework but the state of consciousness is not seriously questioned. Certain people, of course, who are thought to be mad, are said to need their consciousnesses changing. The proposed change, however, is one from a deviant to a normal state. To go further and challenge the state of normalcy itself may even be taken as a sign of madness.

Let me summarize the discussion in simple terms. I have considered the possibilities of a two stage initiation. Stage one would be that which we regard as education in the most general sense, either formal or informal, direct or indirect. As such it may be thought of as a cure for ignorance. The second stage would be a cure for education in the sense that it offered the possibility of a fundamental change in consciousness, an adult initiation. It would be absurd, even sinister, to think that these two stages could be formalized as part of a guided desirable development for human beings. Theodore Roszak may have had something like this in mind when he refers to the dangers of the Human Potentials Movement. In the latter, therapy is a form of mysticism using yogic and Taoist sources but without the metaphysical commitments of religion. Roszak warns that;

> it can end in a kind of splendid psychosensory athleticism, with all the emotional knots untied and the kinks carefully smoothed away . . . . They tune their psyches with marvellous self-indulgence

until there is not an inhibition, not a frustration
left to ruffle their calm. They are much like the
body-builders who fastidiously train every last
little muscle and tendon to perfection. . . . Perhaps
someday we shall have a National Psychic Development Competition with awards for Mr. and
Miss Ataraxy. . . . But what was the warning the
wise Zen master gave his pupil? 'Now that you
have achieved total perfection enlightenment, you
may expect to be just as miserable as ever.'[230]

It is possible, therefore, to imagine circumstances where the
second stage would be domesticated and simply be an exten-
sion of the first. But there is a sense in which the second must
always appear subversive to the first stage. My own view,
implied throughout much of the discussion so far, is that no
radical transformation – which the religions speak about in
their different ways – is conceivable without the possibility of
a second stage. Without this the religions are – again, in their
different ways – simply *rubbing in* the conventions of stage
one. Needless to say the so called secular view not only rests
within stage˙ one but belongs to it by definition and has no
stage beyond.

The chapter so far could read like a put down for what we
normally call the everyday conventional world. This would
be unfortunate. I am not arguing that the conventional state
of consciousness is empty. On the contrary, it contains great
possibilities of depth, insight and feeling. Take as a simple
example, the artistic convention of depth in a picture. If I look
at a picture and see depth in it, as I would were I watching the
actual scene it depicts, my senses are being dominated by an
idea. The convention of perspective is taking primacy over
what is actually there to be seen, namely, paint on a flat
canvas. Yet the convention of perspective gives the painted
area depth and beauty. Nevertheless, the perspective is also
part of what is there to be seen and there is no reason why I
should not see it for what it is – a conventional way of

creating a particular sense of reality. It is quite another matter to be completely taken in by the perspective. Imagine a life size scene painted in perspective on a wall. If expertly done I might attempt to walk into it. This would be a particularly dramatic way of waking up to the fact that I had not 'seen through' a convention.

DAYLIGHT CONSCIOUSNESS

The first stage in the development of consciousness can be compared to a journey on the circumference of a circle. The second stage is a journey to the centre. Any point on the circumference is the same distance from the centre. From the centre, any event on the circumference may be seen in the same centred, transformed way. In my own experience, many people, once exposed to the kind of thought found in the writings of Krishnamurti, for example, see how we are indeed in the grip on the *known*. It can be a very disorientating experience. It is as though they had, as it were, one foot in the centre and the other on the circumference. One half of them is at ease in the eternal now; the other half is still chasing shadows on the circumference. What can be done about it? How do we become the still point in a turning world? If the problem is seen in religious terms the religious solutions will be appropriate. The problem may be spoken of in terms of the absent God. If only God were real. The religious ways of sensing the presence of God would speak to this condition. But what if the problem is not seen in such terms? It is tempting to think that there must be a *direct* remedy compared with which the religious solution is *analogical*. This is simply not possible. There is no language or conceptual system available which is able to speak about reality as it *is*. There is no objective way of speaking, no conceptual method or tool external to ourselves which we can use to trans-form ourselves. Let me make the point by adapting an image once used by Ramana Maharshi. Concepts for breaking through form and multiplicity, whether they be the 'I' or the 'Self' are like the sticks used to poke the funeral pyre. In India the men responsible for making sure that the whole body is burned use sticks to stir the ashes for the incineration to be complete. The sticks *too* are then thrown into the fire. There can be no non-religious concepts which are less combustible than the religious ones. The big sticks of the philosophers and sociologists go into the fire too. If the reality of God is above and beyond the idea of God, then so must any reality about which the non-religious concepts speak be beyond those concepts.

It is true that a great deal of contemporary theology written in the last twenty years has been seduced by the thought that the reality once expressed through the now impotent symbols of religion could be more directly expressed in non-religious categories. Bonhoeffer's cryptic prison utterances about the non-religious interpretation of biblical concepts provided the inspiration for the theological capitulation to the critical canons of the secular outlook. Some theologians succumbed totally[231] but the idea that the world is fundamentally ordinary and secular to be interrupted – where possible – by religious experience is a dogma which haunts much modern theology.

Let me return now to the plight of those who feel themselves to be in the grip of the known. It seems that there is no clean cut way of thinking which we can adopt in order to prize ourselves free. We may feel that traditional religious ways of thinking distance us from reality but even the most contemporary and secular ideas do not tell how and what the world *is*, free from ideas *about* it – the known. We may realize that ideas cannot cut away ideas and yet still feel the urge to ask Krishnamurti's 'impossible' question; how can the mind free itself from the known? Is it something I can do? Can well-intentioned 'I' trans-form hypnotized 'me'? We can try but every effort seems to end in frustration. To use R.H. Blyth's image; we are just about to swat the fly when it flies up and lands on the swatter. Ram Dass comes to this conclusion;

Sooner or later the realization comes that nothing you can think of is going to do it. Nothing you experience is it. Because your mind thinks of things and you and the thing are separate and there is a little veil, like a trillionth of a second that exists between you and the thing you're thinking of. And when you sense something or collect an experience, there's the distinction between the experience and the experiencer and that's a very thin veil. It doesn't matter how thin it is, it's like steel. It always separates you from where it's happening.[232]

We can never be an object to ourselves and, therefore, whatever we think *about* ourselves – I, me – is a lie we tell ourselves, always only an idea. It is strange to say, however, that we would not realize that this were the case if we did not try and fail. The attempt at self-improvement is exactly an expression of the state of illusion. The desire to be enlightened is an appetite of the deluded self. But it tells us something. In one of his lectures Alan Watts observes how water behaves when thrown on to uneven ground. It sends out fingers and rolls back if the slope is too steep. Suppose the water could speak. Would it groan to itself, 'I've failed,' as it rolled back down? Watts comments that we would certify such water as neurotic. The ground is simply telling the water the way things are. The water is behaving naturally. Similarly, our attempts to do what is impossible tell us something. Transformation is not to be realized that way. What then is the way? One answer could be to *watch*. Simply observe what is going on without attempting to classify and judge. Many will feel this to be an impossible demand. We are compulsive thinkers, translating direct experience into symbols. However, it is possible to listen to our thoughts as we would listen to traffic noise, that is, just as noise. In this state we would be observing our 'inward' thoughts in the same way that we normally think of ourselves observing the 'external' world; treating our 'subjective' feelings and thoughts as 'outward' events. The

classical word for this state is, of course, meditation. This
should not be thought of, however, as a technique to achieve
a goal, something to be gained. Krishnamurti, it will be
recalled, despises meditation as a self-improving method. It
may simply be a subtle form of possessiveness as illustrated in
the story of the professional meditator. A king offered his
yogi the finest horse in the kingdom if he could be buried alive
for a whole year in a state of deep samadhi, beyond the
dualism of self and other. The yogi was duly buried but was
soon forgotten when the country became involved in warfare
and the king was overthrown. The yogi was discovered some
ten years later still in samadhi. He was roused with the sacred
sound 'Om.' The yogi's first words were, 'Where's the horse?'

Krishnamurti's attitude towards meditation looks ambiva-
lent, even paradoxical, at first glance. He is contemptuous of
it as a studied technique yet advocates it as a permanent state
of mind. His writings are a strange phenomenon. Time and
again he directs criticism against meditation. However, the
sympathetic reader unwittingly finds himself meditating in
the course of reading a critique of meditation. The grip of the
known is being subtly prized away as he shows how meditation itself can become a calculated, acquisitive exercise.

What, we may ask, is the aim or purpose of all of this? To
what does it lead? The answers are nothing and nowhere. But
this is not meant in a depressing and nihilistic sense. If
meditation has an aim it is not meditation. A purpose
distracts us from the contemplation of the here and now. Aim
and purpose then are the wrong words. Perhaps 'sense of it' is
better. The sense of it is to see the world simply as it is, what
Mahayana Buddhists call its *suchness*, 'tathata' in Sanskrit.
Seen in this way, the world or life is not a problematic thing
being confronted by a subjective presence called 'I' or 'me.' 'I'
am not a separate reality. There is awareness, of course. As
William James observed, 'I' is a term of position, meaning
'awareness here.' It is an awareness totally centred in reality
rather than an entity 'facing up' to it. Thought beguiles us into
the sensation that we are actually confronting the world. To
quote Ram Dass again;

Thoughts keep clothing themselves in all kinds of
silk and glitter and they say, 'I'm not just another
thought...I'm *you*.' You know. 'I'm *real*. This
judgment is the real thought.' But it's just another
thought. This whole game is just thought.[233]

To pick up an image I used earlier, the thoughts we have
about ourselves belong to the circumference of the circle, the
closed system of tram rail where we have thoughts about
thoughts about thoughts. From the centre of the circle the
circumference may appear magical rather than vicious. The
circle is an old image of the eternal and, in religious terms, the
awareness I am describing is that of the eternal now, seeing
life from the centre, *sub specie aeternitatis*. A concrete image
may fill this out a little. Some readers may be familiar with
the 'ghost cradle' ride found in large fun fares. Imagine a large
cradle or boat open at front and rear. Inside two benches are
fitted along the two sides of it so that two small groups of
people sit facing each other. The cradle is suspended above
floor level so that it can swing from side to side. The ride
takes place indoors in a small room. The cradle begins to
swing one way so that one set of people are almost to the
ceiling looking down at the other group who are near the
floor looking up. No safety belts are fitted yet no one drops
out on to the people below. The cradle then swings the
opposite way. The effect is totally disorientating. The
explanation is actually quite simple. It is the room itself which
turns, not the cradle which swings. Once this is realized the
feeling of total confusion dissolves. The sensation can,
therefore, be experienced either way. I may feel myself being
swung around the room. Alternatively, I may just sit and
watch the room revolve.

This is a very simple illustration on a purely physical plane
of two possible states at the level of consciousness itself.
Totally centred awareness, life in the eternal now – call it
what you will – is always in the same relation to any point on
the circumference. There are varying distances between
points on the circumference but they are always the same

distance from the centre. Put into what we usually call practical terms it means something like this. The world as normally experienced appears to be on its way somewhere. Some may think that it is going to destroy itself. Others may believe that it has a more promising destiny. Either way, it has some kind of career and a history. In more personal terms, it is the sense we have when we feel that life is getting later and later. People commonly talk about living *from* day *to* day. By contrast, centred awareness sees time as an illusion and merely a way of measuring motion. There is movement, certainly, but it is not like that of a train moving *along* a track. Rather, it is as though everything were pouring *into* this moment. There is life and motion but the world is simultaneously at its goal. Normal awareness categorizes one area of experience – like a spotlight in darkness – and is seduced into thinking that it is somehow incomplete and isolated. It is, however, our way of attending to it which creates the sense of fragmentation. By contrast, centred awareness – call it daylight rather than spotlight – realizes that the separations are purely conceptual. In reality, everything goes together. What is isolated by spotlight at night is not so by day.

There are hints in so-called everyday experience which suggest what totally centred awareness could be like. Children are often so absorbed in play that they do not notice distinctions which are obvious to adults. I recall a parent once telling me about his son who returned home one evening to say he had found a new playmate. His father asked whether the friend was a black African or a white European. His son simply replied that he had not noticed. Such experiences, however, are not unknown to adults. Car drivers frequently arrive at traffic lights, for example, and suddenly realize that they cannot remember driving the previous mile or so. They responded to all the hazards but did not experience them as separate and serialized events. The approach to knowledge and learning in the West is based on the product of stored, serialized conscious attention. Knowledge is memory. It creates the feeling that the world is all bits and pieces or all 'spots and jumps' to use Bertrand Russell's phrase. This may have been in the mind of Clutton Brock when he said that science tells a lot of little truths in the interest of a great lie and that religion tells a lot of little lies in the interest of a great truth. To concentrate on bits and pieces – even to have such categories – may create the impression or 'lie' that reality *is*, in fact, a *collection* of bits and pieces. Several years ago a puppet character, Torchy the battery boy, was created for children's television. He wore a type of miner's helmet which projected a narrow torchlight beam in front of him. This is a simply image of the way in which we consciously attend to the world. Our education creates a 'torchy' way of knowing which is, paradoxically, a form of ignorance. We ignore the non-dual or undifferentiated nature of the world and think that conceptual categories represent real distinctions.

Another simple example of the difference between certain states of consciousness is suggested by comparing a film to a play. In an interview shortly before his death the actor Ralph Richardson commented on the differences between these two forms of drama. One of his observations casts some light on the centred kind of consciousness which I have attempted to discuss in this chapter. The completed film, he says, by its very nature flows relentlessly on. The characters are encapsulated in a drama which follows a predetermined course. It is in the 'can.' The play often seems to run just as relentlessly for the actor. Richardson said that the play begins and it is as though an iron ball is running down an incline. One character says his lines and they call for a rehearsed response. Yet he observed how a great actor or actress by subtle use of timing could, and often must, 'stop' the play and see the drama as complete at that moment, although from a temporal point of view the drama still has time to run.

To be free from the known is in some way to see the world as the actor sees the drama in such moments. The world appears an essentially mysterious and unspeakable reality. Other people too are just as mysterious when we experience them free from the known categories and roles. It is as though one were to say to another, 'Let us relate to each other now as though we had no ideas about what *should* happen.' If someone finds the world in general essentially ordinary, surprise free, they are hardly likely to find a single human being mysterious, except for a short time. Erich Fromm, in *The Art of Loving*,[234] describes how we find mystery in the beloved which pales all too quickly. We move on only for the same thing to happen again and again. However, we could add to Fromm's comments and say that the beloved is *always* mysterious. We become bored by our own ideas *about* them. In their 'suchness' they are as fascinating as ever.

There is a Zen-like story which illustrates the tendency to impose purpose and role on the mysterious suchness of the other. A man stood on a hill. Three men were out walking and notice the man in the distance. They began to argue about the man's purpose in standing there. One said, 'He has probably lost his dog.' The second disagreed; 'No, he's probably out looking for a friend.' The third said, 'He's only standing up there to enjoy the fresh air.' The three could not agree and were still arguing by the time they approached the man himself. The first man asked him, 'Tell me, have you lost your dog?' 'No sir,' was the reply, 'I have not lost him.' Another asked, 'Have you lost your friend?' 'No sir, I have not lost my friend either.' Finally, the third man asked, 'Are you here to enjoy the fresh air?' 'No, sir.' 'What, then, *are* you standing here for since you answer no to all our questions?' The man said, 'I'm just standing.'

LIVING LIGHTLY ON THE EARTH

I said in an earlier part of the book that this chapter was intended for those who had no particular religious view. It is obvious, however, that anyone who has taken the trouble to read it will actually have come to it with philosophical views about the world. Non-religious they may be said to be but they will, nevertheless, be views of some kind. Secular and materialist outlooks are often thought to be the opposites of religious beliefs. In the context of the present study this would be a mistaken way of putting the matter. The issue is often expressed in that way because it is assumed that religious people do have *beliefs* but that secular minded people do not. I hope it is clear by now that the secular and materialist outlooks are themselves beliefs. If we *insisted* on talking about opposites to religious beliefs, the opposing position would be that of having no view at all, rather than the secular view. But is such a thing possible? The Taoist approach, which I have mentioned from time to time, comes close to this possibility. It is the approach which the Western religions and secular views need to heed perhaps more than any other. There is a Taoist saying that the scholar gains every day while the Tao man loses everyday. This is not to say that the Tao man becomes progressively moronic. It means, rather, that he does not have fixed ideas about the world. He sees the true status of ideas. There are clouds in the sky and thoughts and ideas in consciousness. He does not mistake the conceptual description of the world with the world itself. By contrast, those who cannot see through this fallacy imagine that the world, to use Paul Tillich's phrase, is a totally calculable object. Thought may even be experienced as superior to the real world which seems a clumsy copy by comparison. What is possible to thought is impossible in nature. As the Taoist view shows so vividly, all imaginable polarities are inseparable in the real world. They arise mutually. However, the dualistic medium of language and thought beguiles us into thinking that the distinctions of the mind correspond to distinctions in reality, that cause is separable from effect, positive from negative, as though a controlling ego could choose to retain the yang and reject the yin.

As we have seen, one of the central aims of Alan Watts' philosophical output was to interpret the Taoist outlook as a viable option for the West. Watts, like many other people, found it almost impossible to be a Christian out of doors. The traditional forms of Christian thought seemed so contrary to the forms of nature. Nevertheless, Watts and other writers[235] have suggested ways in which Christianity can become sensitive to the Taoist vision. Christians may then behave less like those who 'have dominion' and, to use Gary Snyder's words, learn 'to live lightly in the earth.' Before moving into a conclusion it may be appropriate to mention Aldous Huxley again. Towards the beginning of this book I referred to his comments about the clutter, linguistic and otherwise, which reduce our awareness. Towards the end of his life Huxley seems to have been true to his own philosophy when he expressed his emotions about a Californian brushfire which destroyed his home and a lifetime's possessions. A journalist asked him how he felt. Huxley replied, 'I feel clean.'

Conclusion
Into every life a little Zen must fall

IN SOME WAYS THIS book has been written for those who are half in or half out of a religious tradition, but also for any who wonder to themselves about the kind of myth they occupy. For those who think they have no myths, I have nothing more to say. The questioning spirit I have tried to write for is well expressed by Carl Jung when he asked himself;

> In what myth does man live nowadays? In the Christian myth? Do you live in it? Then do we no longer have any myth? But then what is your myth – the myth in which you do live.[236]

One of the best ways of answering this question is to allow a little Zen to fall. I have developed this suggestion through the writings of Alan Watts and Krishnamurti, but what it really all amounts to is this. If we suspend our standardized conceptual approach to the world, we may well see a very different world compared with that we see through the venetian blinds of our own particular myth. Put in a matter of fact way, it is not knowledge or information we need so much as clarity. In religious terms, it is not revelation so much as a new state of consciousness. What is important for the view I have discussed throughout this book is not the right doctrine but the attainment of the true experience. It is giving up believing in belief.

These suggestions would, I think, go against the grain for many a theologian. They are very problem centred persons these days. Their struggle is very much a conceptual one. In theological circles there is often present the feeling that things would be better if some person or group refined our ideas of God to match the modern critiques. Perhaps a charismatic intellectual – a new Bonhoeffer – will write a book or a more modest scholar will create a breakthrough with the umpteenth reinterpretation of Hegel or Karl Barth. If the theologians would give up this particular chase occasionally, they might see their task in a quite different way. If they suspended their obsession with concepts, they would see their own thoughts and ideas as themselves gestures in the world as natural as flowers. This approach implies a new kind of theological critique which is in embryo in Alan Watts' writings. Like the ministers who can see through their own religion, the theologians who can see through their own theology will become more imaginative, even poetic. If they are daring enough to see through the conventional descriptions of the world, they may well have a new sense of the God who transcends the descriptions. This new sense cannot come by a refinement of ideas and concepts of God. It may come if these ideas become transparent to their consciousness. After all, our idea of God is just that – an *idea*. We need the *feeling* or experience of God before the bookkeeping side of ourselves puts him onto 'automatic.' We need the unremembered God. The word 'need' is not the right word, of course. I am simply trying to distinguish between the unremembered and the theological God. If the reader objects and says that both of these are *ideas*, I can only agree and hope that they have seen the point of the previous chapters.

What then are we to answer to Jung's question; 'In what myth does man live nowadays?' Some would answer, I know, that truly contemporary people do not have myths. We are open-minded and scientific in our approach to reality. This, I believe, is the myth in which we live nowadays. The belief that we have no myths is precisely the myth. If there is anything worthwhile to be found the scientist will find it. So goes the myth. A few individuals can see cracks in the current scientific paradigm and some, like Gary Zukav, say that we may be approaching 'the end of science.' The grip of the myth, however, has a stranglehold on many modern cultures. Ludwig Wittgenstein was once commenting to Rush Rhees on the fallacy of thinking that the Marxist revolution would be more penetrating if it enlisted the aid of science. Wittgenstein went on; 'In fact, nothing is more *conservative* than science. Science lays down railway tracks. And for scientists it is important that their work should move along those tracks.' Rhees observes that 'Wittgenstein spoke at other times of "railway tracks" as the image behind the way some people thought and spoke of "scientific laws" or "natural necessity"; or...."scientific method." '[237] The status of ideas and symbols in the western humanist and scientific myths does not exactly encourage the kind of direct apprehension of reality of which the religions are analogical expressions. If we *want* to see religion in problematic terms, this is *the* problem. The analogies can hardly appear rich and evocative to people who have no feeling of transformed identity and consciousness. If people do agree with this assessment, some of them may feel that we should do something about it. But this sounds too much like a serious task for religion, another shadow to chase. I do not know what to do about it in the same way that the ferryman, Vasudeva, could not tell Hermann Hesse's Siddhartha about the 'other thing.' Siddhartha tries to learn it from a great variety of sources – doctrines, teachers, ascetics, a rich merchant, a dice player and a beautiful courtesan. He learns it, eventually, from the river which most travellers saw merely as an obstacle to their journey. As he nears the end of his quest, Siddhartha listens as the ferryman talks of the wisdom of the water;

> 'You have already learned from the river that it is good to strive onwards, to sink, to seek the depths. The rich and distinguished Siddhartha will become a rower; Siddhartha the learned Brahmin will become a ferryman. You have also learned this from the river. You will learn the other thing too.'

After a long pause, Siddhartha said: 'What
other thing, Vasudeva?'

Vasudeva rose. 'It has grown late,' he said, 'let
us go to bed. I cannot tell you what the other thing
is, my friend. You will find out, perhaps you
already know. I am not a learned man; I do not
know how to talk or think. I only know how to
listen and be devout; otherwise I have learned
nothing.'[238]

At the beginning of this book, I mentioned the tortured,
doubt-racked philosophical theologian on Arnold's Dover
Beach. Siddhartha, listening to the river, presents a very
different picture. He contemplates the eternal now and the
other thing – the illusion of time. What would the sage and
the theologian have to say to each other? Their discussion
would, I think, resemble that between the father and the son
in the old Sufi story. The father tries to explain that his son is
suffering from double vision. The son protests, 'How can I be
seeing double, father? There would be four moons up there
instead of two.' Siddhartha would have to overcome the theologian's double vision and show that the idea and the reality
are not separate things. If the theologian pressed to ask what
is *meant* by the eternal now, we can imagine Siddhartha's
reply; 'Here it is. Look at it.'

Let Alan Watts have the last word;

It is ridiculous to try to be so inhuman as never to
feel any regrets about the passing of time and of
life. It is likewise inhuman not to have the paradise fantasy of the mysterious place around the
corner, just over the crest of the hill, just behind
the island in the distance. Because that place is
really the big joke: that's *you!* That's why you
have found that at the end of the line, when you
get to...the last stairway, you are likely to be

confronted with a mirror. And so everybody is seeking, seeking, seeking for that thing that you've just got to have. Well *you've* got it! But nobody's going to believe this, but there it is, the real thing that you are looking for at the end of the line.

And it is far, far more reliable than any kind of external scene which you could love and cling to and hold on to. But of course the whole fascination of life is that that seems perfectly incredible...that mystery, that deep, deep, ever so deep thing which is before all worlds, is you, the unrecognized self.[239]

Bibliography 1
The works of Alan Watts

The following list of books and articles, in chronological order, is not complete but does contain most of Alan Watts' written output. The editions mentioned are those used in the course of the present book.

BOOKS

The Legacy of Asia and Western Man, (London: John Murray, 1937).

Time and Convention, six broadcasts over Station KPFA, (San Francisco: Alan Watts, 1956).

Easter: Its Story and Meaning, (London: Abelard-Schuman, 1959).

The Spirit of Zen, A way of life, work and art in the Far East, (New York: Grove, 1960).

The Way of Zen, (Harmondsworth: Penguin, 1962).

Psychotherapy East and West, (New York: Mentor, 1963).

The Joyous Cosmology, Adventures in the chemistry of consciousness, (New York: Vintage, 1965).

Nonsense, (San Francisco: Stolen Paper Editions, 1967).

The Meaning of Happiness, The Quest for freedom of the Spirit in Modern Psychology and the Wisdom of the East, (London: Village Press, 1968).

Myth and Ritual in Christianity, (Boston: Beacon Press, 1968).

Does It Matter?, Essays on man's relation to materiality, (New York: Pantheon, 1970).

Behold the Spirit, A study in the necessity of mystical religion, (New York: Vintage, 1971).

Erotic Spirituality: The Vision of Konarak, with photographs
by Eliot Elisofon, (New York: Collier Macmillan, 1971).

The Supreme Identity, An essay on oriental metaphysic and
the Christian religion, (London: Wildwood House, 1973).

Beyond Theology, The art of Godmanship, (New York:
Vintage, 1973).

Nature, Man and Woman, (London: Wildwood House,
1973).

In My Own Way, An autobiography 1915-1965, (New York:
Vintage, 1973).

The Book on the Taboo Against Knowing Who You Are,
(London: Sphere, 1973).

The Wisdom of Insecurity, (London: Rider, 1974).

The Essence of Alan Watts, single lectures published in
booklet form on the following subjects: God, Philosophical
Fantasies, Death, Meditation, Nothingness, The Nature of
Man, Time, Cosmic Drama, Ego, (California: Celestial
Arts, 1974/75). Some of these talks, together with a few
previously unpublished lectures, have been printed as one
volume in

The Essential Alan Watts, (California: Celestial Arts,
1977).

Cloud-Hidden, Whereabouts Unknown, a mountain journal,
(London: Sphere, 1977).

The Is It, and other essays on Zen and spiritual experience,
(London: Rider, 1978).

The Two Hands of God, The Myths of Polarity, (London:
Rider, 1978).

Uncarved Block, Unbleached Silk, The Mystery of Life, with
photographs by Jeff Berner, (New York: A & W Publishers,
1978).

Tao: The Watercourse Way, with the collaboration of Al
Chung-Liang Huang, (Harmondsworth: Penguin, 1979).

Om: Creative Meditations, edited by Judith Johnstone,
(California: Celestial Arts, 1980).

Play to Live, Selected Seminars edited by Mark Watts,
(Indiana: And Books, 1982).

The Way of Liberation, Essays and Lectures on the transformation of the self, edited by Mark Watts and Rebecca Shropshire, (New York & Tokyo: Weatherhill, 1983).

ESSAYS AND INTERVIEWS

'The Rusty Swords of Japan.' *Asia*, May 1939, New York.

'How Buddhism Came To Life.' *Asia*, (New York: October 1939).

'The Problem of Faith and Works in Buddhism.' *Review of Religion*, vol 5, (New York: Columbia University, May 1941).

'The Negative Way.' *Vedanta for Modern Man*, ed. Christopher Isherwood, (London: Allen & Unwin, 1952).

'The Language of Metaphysical Experience.' *Journal of Religious Thought*, vol 10, pt 2, (Washington D.C.: Howard University, 1953).

'On Philosophical Synthesis.' *Philosophy East and West*, vol. 3, no 2, (July 1953).

'Oriental "Omnipotence." ' *Tomorrow*, vol 4, pt 1, (New York: 1955).

'Picture without a frame.' *The Middle Way*, vol 31, no 1, (May 1956).

'Convention, Conflict and Liberation.' *American Journal of Psychoanalysis*, vol 16, (1956).

'Asian Psychology and Modern Psychiatry.' *Psychopathology: A Source Book*, eds. C.F. Reed, I.E. Alexander and S.S. Tomkins, (Cambridge: Harvard University Press, 1958).

'The Way of Liberation in Zen Buddhism.' *The Middle Way*, vol 33, no 2, (August 1958).

'The Individual as Man/World.' *The Psychedelic Review*, vol. 1, pt 1, (Cambridge, Mass: June 1963).

'The Innocent Senses.' *The Middle Way*, vol 40, no 2, (August 1965).

A Redbook Dialogue: Shirley Maclaine and Alan Watts. *Redbook*, vol 127, pt 1, (U.S.A.: May 1966.)

'Western Mythology: Its Dissolution and Transformation.' *Myths, Dreams and Religion*, ed. Joseph Campbell, (New York: Dutton, 1970).

'The Deep In View.' *Dust: A Quarterly*, (London: 1970).

'Introduction.' *The Theologia Mystica of St. Dionysius*, trs. by Alan Watts, New York: The Holy Cross Press, 1944. New 'Introduction' in a revised edition, (California: S.C.P. Inc., 1972).

'The Art of Contemplation,' (New York: Pantheon, 1972).

Foreword to Franklin Jones' *The Knee of Listening*, (Clearlake: Dawn Horse Press, 1972).

'The Parable of the Cow's Tale.' The Middle Way, vol 49, no 3, (November 1974).

'Can We Help Ourselves?' *The Middle Way*, vol 51, no 1, (May 1976).

'Divine Madness,' *Lo Letter Quarterly*, vol 1, (California).

There is an Alan Watts Institute based at Mill Valley, California.

Bibliography 2
Other works cited

Titles are listed by author in alphabetical order.

Michael Adam, *Wandering in Eden*, (London: Wildwood House, 1976).

Thomas J. J. Altizer & William Hamilton, *Radical Theology and The Death of God*, (Harmondsworth: Penguin, 1968).

A.J. Ayer, *Language Truth and Logic*, 2nd ed., (London: Gollancz, 1946).

N. Berdyaev, *The Destiny of Man*, (London: Bles, 1937).

Peter L. Berger, *The Heretical Imperative*, (New York: Doubleday, 1979).

Peter L. Berger, Brigitte Berger & Hansfried Kellner, *The Homeless Mind*, (New York: Random House, 1973).

Peter L. Berger & Thomas Luckmann, *The Social Construction of Reality*, (Harmondsworth: Penguin, 1966).

Morris Berman, *The Reenchantment of the World*, (Ithaca & London: Cornell University Press, 1981).

R. H. Blyth, *Oriental Humour*, (Tokyo: Hokuseido Press, 1959).

———, *Zen and Zen Classics*, (New York: Vintage Books, 1978).

David Brandon, *Zen and the Art of Helping*, (London: Routledge & Kegan Paul, 1976).

Joseph Campbell, *The Masks of God: Oriental Mythology*, (Harmondsworth: Penguin, 1976).

John V. Canfield, 'Wittgenstein and Zen,' *Philosophy 50*, (1975).

Fritjof Capra, *The Tao of Physics*, (London: Wildwood House, 1975).

Chosetsu, from *Zen Poems of China and Japan*, trans. L. Stryk, T. Ikemoto & T. Takayama, (New York: 1973).

Harvey Cox, *Turning East*, (New York: Simon & Schuster, 1977).

Don Cupitt, *Taking Leave of God*, (London: SCM, 1980).

_____, *The World to Come*, (London: SCM, 1982).

Arthur C. Danto, *Mysticism and Morality*, (Harmondsworth: Penguin, 1976).

Ram Dass, *Grist for the Mill*, (London: Wildwood House, 1978).

_____, *Be Here Now*, (New Mexico: Lama Foundation, 1971).

William Earle, 'The Death of Culture into Expertise,' in *Public Sorrows and Private Pleasures*, (Bloomington: Indiana University Press, 1976).

Paul Engelmann, *Letters from Ludwig Wittgenstein with a Memoir*, (Oxford: Basil Blackwell, 1967).

K. T. Fann, *Wittgenstein's Conception of Philosophy*, (Oxford: Basil Blackwell, 1969).

Marilyn Ferguson, *The Aquarian Conspiracy*, (London: Granada, 1982).

Erich Fromm, *The Art of Loving*, (London: Allen & Unwin, 1957).

Charles Y. Glock & Robert N. Bellah, eds., *The New Religious Consciousness*, (Berkeley: University of California Press, 1976).

Thaddeus Golas, *The Lazy Man's Guide to Enlightenment*, (New York: Bantam, 1980).

Nelson Goodman, *Ways of Worldmaking*, (Sussex: Harvester Press).

Michael Goulder & John Hick, *Why Believe in God?*, (London: SCM, 1983).

Chris Gudmunsen, *Wittgenstein and Buddhism*, (London: Macmillan, 1977).

Herman Hesse, *Siddhartha*, (London: Pan Books, 1973).

John Hick, *Death and Eternal Life*, (London: Collins, 1976).

_____, Problems ot Religious Pluralism (London: Macmillan, 1985).

Michael Horowitz & Cynthia Palmer, eds., *Moksha*, (Harmondsworth: Penguin, 1983).

Aldous Huxley, *The Doors of Perception*, (London: Granada Panther Books, 1977).

_____, *The Human Situation*, (London: Triad/Granada, 1980).

_____, *The Perennial Philosophy*, (London: Fontana, 1958).

Laura Huxley, *This Timeless Moment*, (California: Celestial Arts, 1968).

A. Janik & S. Toulmin, *Wittgenstein's Vienna*, (London: Weidenfeld & Nicolson, 1973).

W. Johnston, *Still Point*, (New York: Harper & Row, 1971).

C. G. Jung, *Memories, Dreams, Reflections*, ed. A. Jaffe, (London: Collins & Routledge & Kegan Paul, 1963).

_____, *Psychology and Alchemy*, Collected Works, Volume 12, (London: Routledge & Kegan Paul, 1953).

Alan Keightley, *Religion and the Great Fallacy*, (New Horizon, 1983).

_____, *Wittgenstein, Grammar and God*, (London: Epworth, 1976).

J. Krishnamurti, *Beyond Violence*, (New York: Harper & Row, 1973).

_____, *Commentaries on Living: First Series*, (London: Gollancz, 1956).

_____, *Commentaries on Living: Second Series*, (London: Gollancz, 1958).

_____, *Commentaries on Living: Third Series*, (London: Gollancz, 1978).

_____, *Education and the Significance of Life*, (London: Gollancz, 1953).

_____, *The First and Last Freedom*, (London: Gollancz, 1954).

_____, *The Flight of the Eagle*, (New York: Harper & Row, 1973).

_____, *Freedom from the Known*, (London: Gollancz, 1969).

_____, *The Impossible Question*, (London: Gollancz, 1972).

_____, *Krishnamurti's Journal*, (London: Gollancz, 1982).

_____, *Krishnamurti's Notebook*, (London: Gollancz, 1976).

_____, *Letters to Schools*, (Beckenham: Krishnamurti Foundation Trust, 1981).

_____, *Life Ahead*, (Harmondsworth: Penguin, 1970).

_____, *The Only Revolution*, (London: Gollancz, 1970).

_____, *This Matter of Culture*, (Harmondsworth: Penguin, 1970).

_____, *Truth and Actuality*, (London: Gollancz, 1981).

_____, *The Urgency of Change*, (Harmoundsworth: Penguin, 1970).

Marghanita Laski, *Ecstasy*, (London: Cresset Press, 1961).

Timothy Leary, 'The Religios Experience: Its Production and Interpretation,' in *Mystery and Miracle*, ed. Edward F. Heenan, (New Jersey: Prentice Hall, 1973).

Jung Young Lee, *Cosmic Religion*, (New York: Harper & Row, 1973).

Kenneth Leech, *The Social God*. (London: Sheldon, 1981).

Stephen Levine, *A Gradual Awakening*, (London: Rider, 1980).

C. S. Lewis, *Of This and Other Worlds*, (London: Collins, 1982).

John Lilly, *The Center of the Cyclone*, (London: Paladin, 1973).

Emily Lutyens, *Candles in the Sun*, (London: Rupert Hart-Davis, 1957).

Mary Lutyens, *Krishnamurti: The Years Awakening*, (New York: Farrar, Straus & Giroux, 1975).

_____, *Krishnamurti: The Years of Fulfilment*, (London: John Murray, 1983).

Sallie McFague, *Metaphorical Theology*, (London: SCM, 1982).

Norman Malcolm, *Ludwig Wittgenstein: A Memoir*, (London: O.U.P., 1958).

Jacob Needleman, *The Heart of Philosophy*, (London: Routledge & Kegan Paul, 1983).

_____, *Lost Christianity*, (New York: Doubleday, 1980).

_____, *The New Religions*, (London: Allen Lane, 1972).

_____, *A Sense of the Cosmos*, (New York: E. P. Dutton, 1975).

Jacob Needleman & George Baker, eds., *Understanding the New Religions*, (New York: Seabury Press, 1978).

Jacob Needleman & Dennis Lewis, eds., *Sacred Tradition and Present Need*, (New York: Viking Press, 1975).

The New Consciousness Sourcebook, (Berkeley: Spiritual Community Publications), published yearly.

Robert E. Ornstein, *The Psychology of Consciousness*, (Harmondsworth: Penguin, 1975).

D. Z. Phillips, 'Alienation and the Sociologizing of Meaning,' in *The Aristotelian Society Supplementary Volume LIII*, (1979).

_____, *Death and Immortality*, (London: Macmillan, 1970).

_____, *Faith and Philosophical Enquiry*, (London: Routledge & Kegan Paul, 1970).

_____, 'On Wanting to Compare Wittgenstein and Zen,' in *Philosophy 52*, (1977).

_____, *Through a Darkening Glass*, (Oxford: Basil Blackwell, 1982).

Theodore Roszak, *The Making of a Counter Culture*, (London: Faber & Faber, 1970).

_____, *Unfinished Animal: The Aquarian Frontier and the Evolution of Consciousness*, (London: Faber & Faber, 1976).

_____, *Where the Wasteland Ends*, (London: Faber & Faber, 1972).

Rush Rhees, ed., *Recollections of Wittgenstein*, (Oxford: O.U.P., 1984).

Bertrand Russell, *The Scientific Outlook*, (New York: W.W. Norton, 1931).

Isaac Bashevis Singer, *A Little Boy in Search of God*, (New York: Farrer, Straus & Giroux, 1974).

Wilfred Cantwell Smith, *Towards a World Theology: Faith and the Comparative History of Religion*, (London: Macmillan, 1981).

R. Sohl & A. Carr, eds., *Games Zen Masters Play: Writings of R.H. Blyth*, (New York: Mentor, 1976).

George Steiner, 'The Thinking Eye,' in *Encounter*, (May 1967).

Barry Stevens, *Don't Push the River*, (Utah: Real People Press, 1970).

David Stuart, *Alan Watts*, (Radnor, Pennsylvania: Chilton Book Co., 1976).

D. T. Suzuki, *Essays in Zen Buddhism, First Series,* (London: Rider, 1950).

———, *Mysticism: Christian and Buddhist,* (London: Allen & Unwin, 1957).

Charles T. Tart, ed., *Altered States of Consciousness,* (New York: Doubleday, 1972).

———, *States of Consciousness,* (New York: E.P. Dutton, 1975).

Paul Tillich, *The Future of Religions,* (New York: Harper & Row, 1966).

Paul Tillich's speech, *Time Magazine*'s 40th Anniversary Celebration, (May 17th, 1963).

Miguel de Unamuno, *The Agony of Christianity,* transl. A. Kerrigan, (London: Routledge & Kegan Paul, 1974).

Ludwig Wittgenstein, *Lectures and Conversations on Aesthetics, Psychology and Religious Belief,* (Oxford: Basil Blackwell, 1966).

———, *On Certainty,* (Oxford: Basil Blackwell, 1969).

———, *Philosophical Investigations,* (Oxford: Blackwell, 1958).

———, 'Lecture on Ethics,' in *Philosophy Today, No. 1,* (London: Collier Macmillan, 1968).

———, *Tractatus Logico-Philosophicus,* (New York: Humanities Press, 1961).

Barry Wood, *The Magnificant Frolic,* (Philadelphia: Westminster Press, 1970).

Heinrich Zimmer, *Philosophies of India,* ed. Joseph Campbell, (New York: Pantheon Books, 1951).

Gary Zukav, *The Dancing Wu Li Masters,* (London: Rider/Hutchinson, 1979).

Notes

INTRODUCTION

1 Jacob Needleman, *The Heart of Philosophy*, p 8.
2 William Earle, 'The Death of Culture into Expertise,' in *Public Sorrows and Private Pleasures*.
3 Monica Furlong's biography of Watts will published by Heinemann in 1986. The February 1984 edition of the Buddhist journal *The Middle Way* was devoted to short biographical essays on Alan Watts with contributions from Gary Snyder, Monica Furlong, P.M. Eden, M.H. Robins, D.T. Sibley and Douglas Harding. See also an earlier biography by an author writing under the *nom de plume* of David Stuart, *Alan Watts*.
4 Theodore Roszak, *Unfinished Animal: The Aquarian Frontier and the Evolution of Consciousness*.
5 *Unfinished Animal*, p 242.
6 See Charles T. Tart, *States of Consciousness* and *Altered States of Consciousness*, ed. Charles T. Tart.
7 Eds, Jacob Needleman & George Baker, *Understanding the New Religions*, pp xif.
8 *The Heart of Philosophy*, p 3.
9 See Wilfred Cantwell Smith, *Towards a World Theology: Faith and the Comparative History of Religion* and John Hick, *Death and Eternal Life; Problems of Religious Pluralism*.
10 Ludwig Wittgenstein, *Philosophical Investigations*, p 31.
11 *Philosophical Investigations*, p 48.

12 Jacob Needleman, *The New Religions*, p 145.
13 R.H. Blyth, *Zen and Zen Classics*, p 98.
14 R.H. Blyth, *Oriental Humour*, p 79.
15 Heinrich Zimmer, *Philosophies of India*, ed. Joseph Campbell, pp 1,8 and 13.
16 *Philosophies of India*, pp 1f.

CHAPTER 1

17 *Time*, May 17th, 1963, p 69.
18 Thomas J.J. Altizer & William Hamilton, *Radical Theology and the Death of God*, pp 95ff.
19 See Eds. Charles Y. Glock & Robert N. Bellah, *The New Religious Consciousness*.
20 Marilyn Ferguson, *The Aquarian Conspiracy*.
21 *Time*, p 69.
22 See *The New Consciousness Sourcebook*, (Berkeley: Spiritual Community Publications), published yearly.
23 John Lilly, *The Centre of the Cyclone*, frontpiece.
24 *The Centre of the Cyclone*, p 21.
25 Thaddeus Golas, *The Lazy Man's Guide to Enlightenment*, p 30.
26 Alan Watts' foreward to Franklin Jones, *The Knee of Listening*.
27 Stephen Levine, *A Gradual Awakening*, p 78.
28 *A Gradual Awakening*, p 77.
29 Jacob Needleman, *A Sense of the Cosmos*, p 145.
30 Jacob Needleman, *Lost Christianity*.
31 eds. Jacob Needleman & Dennis Lewis, *Sacred Tradition and Present Need*, p 7.
32 Quoted in W. Johnston, *Still Point*, p 173.
33 Quoted in Michael Adam, *Wandering in Eden*, p 11.
34 Joseph Campbell, *The Masks of God: Oriental Mythology*, p 9.
35 Quoted in David Brandon, *Zen and the Art of Helping*, p 16.

CHAPTER 2

36   Aldous Huxley, *The Doors of Perception*, p 20. For a recent collection of Huxley's shorter writings on expanded consciousness, see *Moksha*, eds. Michael Horowitz & Cynthia Palmer.

37   D.Z. Phillips, *Death and Immortality*, p 15.

38   Laura Huxley, *This Timeless Moment*, p 86.

39   J. Krishnamurti, *Commentaries on Living: Third Series*, p 169.

40   Robert E. Ornstein, *The Psychology of Consciousness*, pp 47-48.

41   Mary Lutyens, *Krishnamurti: The Years of Awakening*; Emily Lutyens, *Candles in the Sun*. Mary Lutyens has brought the Krishnamurti story up to date with *Krishnamurti: The Years of Fulfilment*. Krishnamurti and his entourage appear in a less favourable light in this second volume. The references to luxurious apartments, Saville Row clothes and Mercedes cars are bound to confirm the suspicions of some critics that Krishnamurti is merely the philsosophical darling of the jet set and the beautiful people.

42   *Krishnamurti: The Years of Awakening*, p 282.

43   J. Krishnamurti, *Beyond Violence*. p 100.

44   J. Krishnamurti, *The Only Revolution*, p 150.

45   J. Krishnamurti, *The Urgency of Change*, p 186.

46   J. Krishnamurti, *Freedom from the Known*, p 20.

47   This anecdote is mentioned in Harvey Cox's *Turning East*, p 117.

48   *Freedom from the Known*, p 36.

49   *Beyond Violence*, p 55.

50   See J. Krishnamurti, *Commentaries on Living: Second Series*, p 64.

51   Ibid. p 32.

52   *Krishnamurti's Notebook*, p 139.

53   J. Krishnamurti, *The Impossible Question*.

54   J. Krishnamurti, *Letters to Schools*, p 55.

55   *The Urgency of Change*, p 306.

56 J. Krishnamurti, *Commentaries on Living: First Series*, p 99.
57 J. Krishnamurti, *This Matter of Culture*, p 234.
58 N. Berdyaev, *The Destiny of Man*, p 45.
59 *Krishnamurti's Journal*, p 58.
60 *Commentaries on Living: Second Series*, p 125.
61 *Beyond Violence*, p 48.
62 J. Krishnamurti, *The Flight of the Eagle*, p 92.
63 *The Urgency of Change*, p 265.
64 J. Krishnamurti, *Truth and Actuality*, p 48.
65 *The Urgency of Change*, p 292.
66 *The Only Revolution*, p 138.
67 *Commentaries on Living: Second Series*, p 151.
68 *Letters to Schools*, p 66.
69 *This Matter of Culture*, p 187.
70 J. Krishnamurti, *Education and the Significance of Life*, p 40.
71 *Beyond Violence*, p 49.
72 J. Krishnamurti, *The First and Last Freedom*, p 19.
73 J. Krishnamurti, *Life Ahead*, p 151.
74 *Commentaries on Living: Third Series*, p 235.
75 *The First and Last Freedom*, p 281.
76 *The Urgency of Change*, p 173.
77 *The First and Last Freedom*, p 97.
78 *Krishnamurti's Journal*, p 27.
79 *The First and Last Freedom*, p 98.
80 See K.T. Fann, *Wittgenstein's Conception of Philosophy*, p 104.
81 *Philosophical Investigations*, p 103.
82 Ibid. p 47.
83 Ibid. p 85.
84 Chris Gudmunsen, *Wittgenstein and Buddhism*, p 115.
85 Quoted in A. Janik and S. Toulmin, *Wittgenstein's Vienna*, pp 233-34.
86 John V. Canfield, 'Wittgenstein and Zen,' *Philosophy* 50, p.408. See also D.Z. Phillips, 'On Wanting to Compare Wittgenstein and Zen,' *Philosophy* 52, pp 338-43.
87 Ibid. p 405.

88   Chosetsu, from *Zen Poems of China and Japan*, trans. L. Stryk, T. Ikemoto and T. Takayama.

89   Heinrich Zimmer, *Philosophies of India*, pp 26-7.

90   Alan Keightley, *Wittgenstein, Grammar and God*, pp 22-30.

91   Paul Engelmann, *Letters from Ludwig Wittgenstein with a Memoir*, p 7.

92   *The Heart of Philosophy*, p 215.

CHAPTER 3

93   *In My Own Way*, p.6.

94   Ibid. p 72.

95   From a lecture, 'The Relevance of Oriental Philosophy,' included in *The Way of Liberation*, p 48.

96   *In My Own Way*, p 5.

97   Ibid. p 92.

98   Ibid. p 451.

99   From an address, 'Veil of Thoughts', included in *Play to Live*, p 43.

100   *The Joyous Cosmology*, p 78.

101   *Nonsense*; see bibliography.

102   *Psychotherapy East and West*, pp 62-63.

103   Ibid. p 41.

104   *Myth and Ritual in Christianity*, p 59.

105   Ibid. p 236.

106   Aldous Huxley, *The Human Situation*, p 177.

107   *In My Own Way*, p 224.

108   *Does It Matter?*, pp 69-70.

109   *Nature, Man and Woman*, p 3.

110   From a lecture, 'Death, Birth and the Unborn', included in *Play to Live*, p 81.

111   *Myth and Ritual in Christianity*, p 59.

112   *In My Own Way*, p 448.

113   Ibid. p 414.

114   *Myth and Ritual in Christianity*, p 63.

115 Ibid. p 63.
116 *The Supreme Identity*, p 50.
117 Ibid. p 134.
118 *The Wisdom of Insecurity*, p 26.
119 *Myth and Ritual in Christianity*, p 61.
120 Ibid. p 70.
121 *Behold the Spirit*, p 96.
122 *Beyond Theology*, p 221.
123 Alan Watts produced two editions of *The Theologia Mystica of Saint Dionysius* – see bibliography.
124 *Myth and Ritual in Christianity*, p 81.
125 Aldous Huxley, *The Perennial Philosophy*, pp 12-13.
126 *Om: Creative Meditations*, p 146.
127 *Behold the Spirit*, p xxv.
128 *In My Own Way*, p 415.
129 *Beyond Theology*, p 25.
130 Ibid. p 26.
131 Arthur C. Danto, *Mysticism and Morality*, p 9.
132 See Alan Watts' article, 'On Philosophical Synthesis.'

CHAPTER 4

133 *Tao: The Watercourse Way*, p 42.
134 See Don Cupitt's comments in his *The World to Come*, p 18.
135 *Philosophical Investigations*, p 48.
136 Ibid. p 116.
137 Ibid. p 116.
138 Ibid. p 49.
139 Ibid. p 224.
140 Ibid. p 88.
141 Ibid. p 226.
142 Ibid. p 168.
143 D.Z. Phillips' writings in particular analyse the genuinely religious core of a range of subjects; prayer, death and eternal life, duty, love, etc.

144 Ludwig Wittgenstein, *Lectures and Conversations on Aesthetics, Psychology and Religious Belief*, p 72.

145 Ludwig Wittgenstein, *On Certainty*, p 23.

146 *Philosophical Investigations*, p 32.

147 Ibid. p 31.

148 *Religious Studies*, vol.5, 1969.

149 This example derives from Wittgenstein's 'Lecture on Ethics,' the only written material we have from him which was delivered to a lay audience. See *Philosophy Today*, No.1.

150 *Lectures and Conversations*, p 53.

151 *Ludwig Wittgenstein:. Personal Recollections*, p 152.

152 C.S. Lewis, *Of This and Other Worlds*, p 141.

153 Isaac Bashevis Singer, *A Little Boy in Search of God*, p 89.

154 See *Wittgenstein, Grammar and God*, pp 55ff. For a more straightforward discussion of the whole question of confusing the description of the world with the world itself, see Alan Keightley, *Religion and the Great Fallacy*.

155 D.Z. Phillips, *Faith and Philosophical Enquiry*, P.S. See also D.Z. Phillips, *Through a Darkening Glass*, pp 127-129.

156 D.T. Suzuki, *Essays in Zen Buddhism*, First Series, p 140.

157 See Theodore Roszak, *The Making of a Counter Culture*, chapter 7.

158 Alan Keightley, *Religion and the Great Fallacy*, p 44.

159 Marghanita Laski, *Ecstasy*, pp 5-6.

160 Alan Watts, *Erotic Spirituality*, pp 72-3.

161 Bertrand Russell, *The Scientific Outlook*, p 98.

CHAPTER 5

162 Ludwig Wittgenstein, *Tractatus Logico-Philosophicus*, 6.52.

163 *Om: Creative Meditations*, p 130.
164 *The Human Situation*, p 171.
165 *Behold the Spirit*, p 104.
166 *Myth and Ritual in Christianity*, p 66.
167 *The Two Hands of God*, p 15.
168 *Time and Convention*, p 7.
169 *The Two Hands of God*, p 16.
170 Ibid. p 15.
171 *In My Own Way*, p 239.
172 *This Is It*, p 19.
173 Ibid. p 31.
174 See his review article, 'The Thinking Eye,' *Encounter*, May 1967, p 61.
175 Ibid. p 61.
176 Quoted in Sallie McFague, *Metaphorical Theology*, p 55.
177 Quoted in Alan Watts, *Play To Live*, p 93.
178 Ibid. p 94.
179 Ibid. p 94.
180 *The Book on the Taboo Against Knowing Who You Are*, p 130.
181 A.J. Ayer, *Language, Truth and Logic*, 2nd ed. p 118.
182 Ibid. pp 118-119.
183 *Erotic Spirituality*, p 74.
184 *In My Own Way*, p 173.
185 See his article, 'The Language of Metaphysical Experience,' p 133.
186 *This Is It*, p 36.
187 *Behold the Spirit*, p xiv.
188 *Taking Leave of God*, and *The World to Come*.
189 Michael Goulder and John Hick, *Why Believe in God?*, p 109.
190 *The Book on the Taboo Against Knowing Who You Are*, p 18.
191 *Nature, Man and Woman*, p 43.
192 *Om: Creative Meditations*, p 128.

CHAPTER 6

193 *Myth and Ritual in Christianity*, p 67.
194 See *Mysticism: Christian and Buddhist*, chapter 6.
195 *The Wisdom of Insecurity*, p 131.
196 *Beyond Theology*, p 123.
197 C.G. Jung, *Psychology and Alchemy*, Collected Works Vol.12, p 12.
198 See Alan Watts' article, 'Can We Help Ourselves?'
199 See Alan Watts' *Easter: Its Story and Meaning*.
200 *Myth and Ritual in Christianity*, p 231.
201 Miguel de Unamuno, *The Agony of Christianity*, transl. A. Kerrigan, p 124.
202 *The Agony of Christianity*, p 185.
203 Quoted in *In My Own Way*, pp 220-221.
204 *Myth and Ritual in Christianity*, p 61.
205 *The Middle Way*, Vol. XXXV, No. 3, Nov. 1960, p 86.
206 *Philosophy Today*, No. 1, ed. Jerry H. Gill, p 19.
207 *Philosophy Today*, No 1, p 11.
208 Kenneth Leech, *The Social God*, p 30.
209 Harvey Cox, *Turning East*, p 30.
210 Norman Malcolm, *Ludwig Wittgenstein: A Memoir*, p 100.
211 *Ludwig Wittgenstein: A Memoir*, p 100.
212 *Ludwig Wittgenstein: A Memoir*, p 100.
213 *Games Zen Masters Play: Writings of R.H. Blyth*, eds. R. Sohl & A. Carr, p 128.
214 *The Wisdom of Insecurity*, p 119.
215 Paul Tillich, *The Future of Religions*, p 45.
216 Alan Watts, *Uncarved Block, Unbleached Silk*, no page numbers.
217 Barry Stevens, *Don't Push the River*, p 76.
218 *Don't Push the River*, p 49.
219 *In My Own Way*, p 223.
220 *Beyond Theology*, p 163.
221 C.G. Jung, *Memories, Dreams, Reflections*, ed. A. Jaffe, p 96.
222 Ibid. p 52.

CHAPTER 7

223 Nelson Goodman, *Ways of Worldmaking*, p 119.

224 Peter L. Berger, Brigitte Berger & Hansfried Kellner, *The Homeless Mind*, p 16.

225 Peter L. Berger & Thomas Luckmann, The *Social Construction of Reality*, p 127.

226 *The Homeless Mind*, p. 5. Berger in particular is very aware of the limitations of sociological studies and sensitive to the self-understanding of religious believers. This is obviously the case in one of his more recent studies, *The Heretical Imperative*, where he examines the contemporary possibilities of religious affirmation.

227 D.Z. Phillips, 'Alienation and the Sociologizing of Meaning,' in *The Aristotelian Society Supplementary Volume LIII*, 1979, p 97. This article is a vigorous critique of Berger's books.

228 Quoted by Nelson Goodman in *Ways of Worldmaking*, p 96.

229 See Leary's essay, 'The Religious Experience: Its Production and Interpretation,' in *Mystery, Magic and Miracle*, ed. Edward F. Heenan, p 36. Richard Alpert was closely associated with Leary's experiments and gives a full account of how he dropped out of the academic world in his book, *Be Here Now*. Alpert took on the new identity of Ram Dass and, in his *Grist for the Mill*, he gives a vivid description of the helplessness often felt by those who have transcended normal states of consciousness. At a press conference after his dismissal from Harvard he writes, 'I looked around and saw that everybody believed in only one reality to this situation except me, and I remembered, since I'm a clinical psychologist, that that was a definition of insanity' (p 22).

230 Theodore Roszak, *Where the Wasteland Ends*, p 101.

231 See Alan Keightley, *Religion and the Great Fallacy*, chapter 8.

232 Ram Dass, *Grist for the Mill*, p 19.

233 *Grist for the Mill*, p 96.

234 *The Art of Loving*, p 11f.

235 See Jung Young Lee, *Cosmic Religion*, and Barry Wood, *The Magnificent Frolic*. Fritjof Capra's *The Tao of Physics*, is a widely read study which examines the parallels between Taoism and modern physics. *The Dancing Wu Li Masters* by Gary Zukav deals less specifically with the Tao but shares Capra's aim in exploring similarities between eastern mysticism and the new physics. Drawing on the work of Jung, Reich and Bateson, Morris Berman examines the possibility of a consciousness for modern times grounded in man's inseparability from the natural world; *The Reenchantment of the World*.

CONCLUSION

236 C.G. Jung, *Memories, Dreams, Reflections*, ed. A. Jaffe, p 171.

237 Rush Rhees ed., *Recollections of Wittgenstein*, p 202.

238 Herman Hesse, *Siddhartha*, pp 84-85.

239 *Uncarved Block, Unbleached Silk*, no page numbers.